CONFUCIUS
AND CONFUCIANISM

BY RICHARD WILHELM

LATE PROFESSOR OF CHINESE AT THE UNIVERSITY
OF FRANKFORT ON THE MAIN

Translated into English by
GEORGE H. DANTON, PH.D.
and
ANNINA PERIAM DANTON, PH.D.

HARCOURT, BRACE AND COMPANY

NEW YORK

PRINTED IN THE UNITED STATES OF AMERICA
BY QUINN & BODEN COMPANY, INC., RAHWAY, N. J.

Translators' Preface

RICHARD WILHELM, the eminent German Sinologue, was a product of the illustrious Tübinger Stift, which numbered among its graduates such famous Germans as Moerike and D. F. Strauss. He went to China as a missionary in 1899, but soon became one of those who imbibe Chinese culture, rather than one who seeks to superimpose Occidental ideals on the Orient. He was, as many conversations with him showed, an extremist in his attitude toward the Chinese ethos, and toward the impact of Western civilization on China, believing, to an extent rare even among the radically minded, in the right of the Chinese to intellectual, political, aesthetic, and social self-determination. He spent the last years of his life as Professor of Chinese at the city university of Frankfort on the Main, where he was in the process of organizing a Sinological school of the first rank when death took him, at the age of fifty-eight, in March, 1930.

The present work, small as it is, offered two

very distinct problems to the translators. The first part of the book is, in itself, a translation of a section of a Chinese work, *The Historical Records*, by Sse-Ma Ch'ien, from about the turn of the second century B.C. As far as we know, there is no English translation of this book, but there is a French rendering by Chavannes. Wilhelm translated directly from the Chinese, but used Chavannes, including the latter's vast learned apparatus, which often completely swamps the actual text. The problem of the translators was, of course, to render Wilhelm, but we discovered that to treat Wilhelm's text without reference to the Chinese original would result in an English rendering which was very apt to be a long remove from what Sse-Ma had said. We therefore collated Wilhelm with the Chinese text in an edition of 1742, lent by the Library of Congress, and with Chavannes, including the notes. We have always actually translated Wilhelm, but when there was any question, we have added translators' notes to explain a few points which Wilhelm takes for granted, or where a mere translation of the German would not be clear. Besides the work of Sse-Ma, Wilhelm has numerous cross references to the Confucian classics, where biographical data on the Sage are found. Here, in every case, we have checked with the Chinese text and have consulted the standard English translation by Legge. Where we have quoted Legge, it is with the intention of indicating the contrast between the colourful and individualistic rendition of Wilhelm and the soberer and sometimes more literal version of the Englishman. Wilhelm, in his translations, often breaks with tradition; our notes are intended to guide the casual reader back to the conventional version, should he care to continue his reading along these lines.

The second problem was the obvious one which every translator meets of rendering his author's style. Wilhelm, contrary to usual German practice in scientific works, writes extremely simply and paratactically. His style is not, in this work, consciously archaistic, but at times it falls into what is almost an archaic rhythm; it is utterly different from the staccato of much contemporary German prose. What is more, Wilhelm tends to invest the austerity of classical Chinese with a certain naïve warmth which is almost untranslatable and which at times, as it seems to us, departs from the mood of classical Chinese. Here again, we have tried to translate Wilhelm, though we are conscious that so distinct a stylist as he can be enjoyed only in the original. That he was a German stylist of delicacy and charm, even those who disagree with some of his scientific opinions are more than ready to admit.

The romanization used is not that of Wilhelm, but of Wade. For those who do not have access to a discussion of this system, it may be of help to note that the vowels have continental values; ê = u as in *but;* o is a diphthong = uo, very short; the syllables *shih, chih, sze, tse, tze,* etc., are pronounced almost without final vowel; the ‘ after p, t, k, ch, indicates the ordinary voiceless English pronunciation; without the inverted apostrophe, the pronunciation is voiced and approximates b, d, g, and j as in *jaw; jen* is pronounced *almost* like *ren.* These, of course, are only very rough approximations. No account is taken of the tonal values of the Chinese words.

The Library of Congress, the Columbia University Library, especially through the kindness of the Chinese curator, Mr. W. Y. Yen, and Mr. Edwin Shui of Oberlin College have been of assistance and are hereby thanked.

For the sake of reference, it may be added that Wilhelm's book is number 979 of the well-known Sammlung Göschen.

A. P. D.
G. H. D.

Oberlin, Ohio
December, 1930

Contents

CONTENTS

CONFUCIUS AND CONFUCIANISM

Chapter I

THE LIFE OF CONFUCIUS, ACCORDING TO THE HISTORICAL ACCOUNTS OF SSE-MA CH'IEN [1]

CONFUCIUS was born in the State of Lu, in the District of Ch'ang P'ing, in the city of Chou. His ancestor was from the State of Sung and was called K'ung Fang-shu. Fang-shu begat Po-hsia. Po-hsia begat Shu-Liang Ho. Late in life, Ho was united in matrimony with the daughter of the man, Yen, and begat Confucius. His mother prayed to the hill, Ni, and conceived Confucius. It was in

[1] *Translators' Note.* The *Shih Chi* of Sse-Ma Ch'ien has been translated into French as *Les mémoires historiques de Se-Ma Ts'ien traduits et annotés par Edouard Chavannes*, Paris, 1905. The life of Confucius is found in Chapter XLVII, pp. 282 ff. Both Wilhelm and Chavannes follow the general tendency among Sinologues in referring to Confucius as K'ung Tze. As will be seen from the text, K'ung is his family name; the Tze is a usual designation among the Chinese for *master, philosopher,* etc. Thus also Lao Tze, where Lao means *old.* The *style* or appellation (Chinese *hao*) is the literary designation; as his cognomen, Ch'iu, has become a sacred word and is therefore tabu, Confucius is referred to by his literary designation, Chung Ni. The word Chung means: the second born of brothers; Confucius was regarded as the second born, the hill Ni being held as the elder.

3

the twenty-second year of Duke Hsiang of Lu
that Confucius was born (551 B.C.). At his birth,
he had on his head a bulging of the skull, whence
he is said to have received the name "Hill"
(Ch'iu). His style or appellation was Chung Ni,
his family name K'ung. When he was born, his
father, Shu-Liang Ho, died. He was buried on
the mountain Fang. The mountain Fang lies
eastward from Lu. Therefore Confucius was in
doubt as to the place of the grave of his father;
for his mother kept silence toward him regarding it.

Confucius was always wont to set up sacrificial
vessels in his childish play, and to imitate ceremonial gestures. When the mother of Confucius
died, he buried her temporarily near the Way of
the Five Fathers, so great was his circumspection.
When the mother of Wan Fu of Chou later in-
structed Confucius concerning the place of the
grave of his father, he went thither and buried the
two bodies together on the mountain of Fang.

While Confucius was still wearing mourning,
Baron Chi gave a banquet for the notables. Confucius also attended. Then Yang Hu took him to

task, and said: "Baron Chi has prepared a banquet for the notables; he has not the honour of inviting you." Thereupon, Confucius withdrew.

When Confucius was seventeen years old, the Minister Mêng Hsi-tze of Lu fell ill, and was nigh unto death.[1] Then he summoned his heir, I-tze, and said: "K'ung Ch'iu is the descendant of a philosopher who was slain in Sung. His ancestor, Fu Fu Ho, had the first claim to the throne of Sung, and as heir he yielded to Duke Li. Chêng Ch'ao-fu[2] was then serving the Dukes Tai, Wu, and Hsüan. Thrice he received ever higher honours, and became therefrom but the more modest. Thus he wrote upon his tripod: 'On the occasion of the first honour, I bowed my head; at the second, I bent my shoulders; and at the third, I walked stooped over. I slink along the wall; thus no one ventures to cast blame upon me. In this utensil I cook my porridge; in it I cook my grits, to still my hunger.' So filled with modesty was he. I have heard that the descendants of a philosopher,

[1] In reality, Mêng Hsi-tze did not die until 518 B.C., when Confucius was thirty-four years old.

[2] *Translators' Note.* Chavannes: *"arrière petit fils de Fu Fu Ho."*

5

even when they do not find a suitable position in their own times, yet finally attain their goal. Now K'ung Ch'iu is still young and loves decorum. Might he be the one for whom success is destined? When I am no more, you must take him as your teacher."

When then Mêng Hsi-tze had died, I-tze and Nan-Chung Ching-shu of Lu went to him to learn decorum of him.

In the same year, Baron Chi Wu died, and P'ing Tze was put in his place. Confucius was poor and of low estate, and when he grew older he served as a petty official of the family Chi, and while he was in office his accounts and the measures were always correct.[1] Thereupon, he was made Chief Shepherd; then the beasts grew in numbers and multiplied.

Therefore he was appointed Minister of Public Works. Finally he left Lu, was abandoned in Ch'i, was driven out of Sung and Wei, suffered want between Ch'ên and Ts'ai. Thereupon he returned to Lu. Confucius was nine feet six inches tall. All

---

[1] The term *petty official* (*Angestellter*) must be used, rather than *scribe* (*Schreiber*). (Cf. Ch'ao Ch'i.)

the people called him a giant and marvelled at him. Lu again treated him well; so he returned to Lu.[1]

Nan-Chung Ching-shu spoke to the Prince of Lu and said: "I crave permission to go with Confucius to Chou." The Prince of Lu gave them a chariot, two horses, and a servant. Thus they went together to Chou (the residence of the Emperor, at Lo Yang, in Honan) and inquired about the rites. In all probability it was at that time that he saw Lao Tze. When Confucius took leave of Lao Tze, the latter, in parting, spoke to him as follows: "I have heard that rich and noble persons make parting gifts; but good people give words in farewell. I am neither rich nor noble, but I am held a good man, so I should like to give you these words upon your way: Shrewd and clever people are near to death, for they love to pass judgment on others. Those who know a great deal and do things on a large scale endanger their persons, for they disclose the mistakes of mankind. He who is the son of another has nothing for him-

[1] This section (i.e., of Sse-Ma Ch'ien) breaks the connection, and anticipates events narrated in detail later on.

self; he who is the official of another has nothing for himself."

After Confucius returned from Chou to Lu, his pupils gradually became more numerous. At this time, Duke P'ing of Chin had given himself over to dissipation, and thus the six noble families had gained control of the government, and were fighting the princes of the land in the east. King Ling of Ch'u possessed a military force with which he oppressed the Middle Kingdom. Ch'i was large and close to Lu. Lu was small and weak. If it yielded to Ch'u, Chin became angry. If it yielded to Chin, Ch'u came to attack it. If it did not arm itself against Ch'i, the armies of Ch'i fell upon Lu.

In the twentieth year of Duke Chao of Lu (522 B.C.), Confucius was about thirty years of age. Duke Ching of Ch'i came to Lu in the company of Yen Ying. Duke Ching interrogated Confucius and said: "In antiquity, Duke Mu of Ch'in was alive; his territory was small and remote. How did it come to pass that he gained the hegemony?" Confucius replied: "Although the State of Ch'in was small, its will was great; although the place was remote, its conduct was simple and correct. The Duke personally raised Po-Li Hsi to the five rams, and ennobled him to the rank of a great official, and elevated him while he was still in chains.[1] He spoke with him for three days; then he gave the reins of government into his hands. In this manner, he himself could have gained control of the royal power. That he obtained nothing more than the hegemony was but little." Duke Ching rejoiced.

When Confucius was thirty-five years old (517 B.C.), Baron P'ing of Chi fell into disfavour with Duke Chao of Lu because of a cock fight with Hou Shao Po. Duke Chao led an army in order to chastize Baron P'ing. But Baron P'ing united with the two other great families, Mêng and Shu-Sun, and together they attacked Duke Chao. The army of Duke Chao was defeated, and he himself fled to Ch'i. And the State of Ch'i har-

[1] *Translators' Note.* Po-Li Hsi (Giles, 1659) was an official whose value the Duke of Ch'in knew. He offered only five rams' skins as a ransom for him, "so as to make it appear that he was an unimportant personage." See also Chavannes, Vol. II, p. 27.

boured Duke Chao in Kan Hou. When, soon after this, disorders arose in Lu, Confucius betook himself to Ch'i, and entered the service of Baron Kao Chao, with the intention of thereby forming a connection with Duke Ching.

He discoursed with the Chief Music-Master of Ch'i on the subject of music. He heard the tones of the Shao music, he learned them, and for three months he forgot the taste of meat.[1]

People of Ch'i spoke of him with praise; Duke Ching thereupon questioned him regarding the government. Confucius said: "Let the prince be prince, the servant servant, the father father, the son son." Duke Ching replied: "That is an excellent answer: if the prince be not prince, and the servant not servant; if the father be not father, and the son not son; even though I have my revenue, how could I enjoy it!"[2]

On another day, he again questioned Confucius about the government. Confucius replied: "Governing consists in being sparing with the resources."

[1] Lun Yü, III, 25; VII, 13.
[2] Lun Yü, XII, 11.

Duke Ching rejoiced, and wished to grant Confucius the fields of Ni Ch'i as a fief. Then Yen Ying interfered and said: "Scholars are smooth and sophisticated; they cannot be taken as a norm; they are arrogant and conceited; they cannot be used to guide the lower classes. They attach a great importance to mourning; they emphasize the lamentations, and waste their substance on magnificent funerals; they cannot be used as regulators of manners. They travel about as advisers in order to enrich themselves; they cannot be used in the ruling of the state. Since the great sages have passed away and the House of Chou has degenerated, rites and music have become defective and incomplete. Now Confucius splendidly forms the rules of behaviour, increases the ceremonies of reception and departure, and the customs in walking and in bowing, so that many generations would not be enough to exhaust his teachings. Years would not suffice to plumb his rules of decorum. If you wish to use him to change the manners of Ch'i, this is not the correct way to lead the common people." After that time, Duke Ching continued to receive Confucius, always, to be sure, with great respect, but he no longer questioned him concerning decorum.[1]

At another time, Duke Ching detained Confucius and said: "I cannot settle such fiefs upon you as have been settled upon the Chi family. I will treat you in a manner that lies between the position of the Chi family and the Mêng family.[2]

The dignitaries of Ch'i wanted to destroy Confucius. Confucius heard of it. Duke Ching said: "I am too old. I can no longer use him." Thereupon, Confucius departed and returned to Lu.

When Confucius was forty-two years old (510 B.C.), Duke Chao of Lu died in Kan Hou. And Duke Ting succeeded him.

After Duke Ting had occupied the throne for five years, Baron P'ing of Chi died during the summer, and Baron Huan succeeded him (505 B.C.).

---

[1] It is not to be supposed that Yen Ying spoke these words, since he was personally friendly to Confucius. The reproaches which are found in the Yen Tse Ch'un Ch'iu, § 8, Wai P'ien, and in Mucius, § 39, Fei Yu, contain, as it were, the arsenal that was constantly used by the opponents of Confucius.

[2] Lun Yü, XVIII, 3.

Baron Huan of Chi dug a well. During the digging they found an earthen vessel which contained something resembling a sheep. They questioned Chung Ni (Confucius), and said: "A dog has been found." Chung Ni said: "According to my opinion, it must be a sheep. The spirits of the trees and stones are *ch'ui* (monopods) and *wang liang;* the spirits of the water are the dragon (*lung*) and *wang hsiang;* the spirit of the earth is the sheep *fên.*[1]

The State of Wu fought the State of Yüeh and destroyed the mountain Kuai Chi (upon which, in the year 494 B.C., the capital of Yüeh was situated). There they found a bone of such a size that it filled an entire wagon. The State of Wu sent a messenger to Chung Ni (Confucius) to ask why the bone was so large. Chung Ni answered: "When Yü assembled all the gods on the mountain Kuai Chi, Fang Fêng arrived too late. Yü had him killed, and exhibited the body. His bones were all so large that they filled a whole wagon. That is why this bone is so large." The stranger

[1] Kuo Yü. Lu Yü 5.

Translators' Note. These are all fabulous animals. And see p. 37, note.

asked: "Who were those gods?" Chung Ni replied: "The gods of the mountains and streams are able to regulate the world. Those to whom sacrifices are made are gods. Those who possess the altars of the earth and of grain are princes.[1] They are all subject to the king." The stranger asked: "What position did Fang Fêng hold?" Chung Ni replied: "He was the prince of Wang Wang, and he had the sacrifices of the mountains Fêng and Yü. He belonged to the clan of Hsi. Under the dynasties of Yü, Hsia and Shang, the land was called Wang Wang; under the Chou Dynasties, it was called 'the long Ti'; today they are called the giants."[2]

The stranger asked: "What is the stature of man's body?" Chung Ni answered: "The Chiao Yao are three feet high; that is the extreme of smallness. The tallest men are at most ten times as tall as this."

[1] *Translators' Note.* Chavannes' translation is clearer: "Those who preside over the sacrifices which are rendered to the soil and the grain are dukes and marquises." The King, as Son of Heaven, ruled over all.

[2] A better reading for Wang Wang is probably Wang Mang, which means *of hybrid origin.*

Translators' Note. The Chinese ideogram in the 1742 edition is *chai*, used for *ti*, and is that applied to certain barbarian tribes.

Thereupon, the stranger of Wu said: "Magnificent! He is a philosopher."

A favorite of Baron Huan, by the name of Chung Liang-huai, was at enmity with Yang Hu. Yang Hu wished, therefore, to drive out Huai. But Kung-Shan Pu-niu prevented him. In the succeeding autumn, Huai was still more arrogant. Then Yang Hu took him prisoner (505 B.C.). Baron Huan grew angry, and Yang Hu imprisoned him. Baron Huan swore an oath; thereupon, he set him free. From that time on, Yang Hu had an ever greater contempt for the House of Chi, while the House of Chi, for its part, usurped the prerogatives of the ducal house. Subordinate vassals had gained the power of the state.[1] Thus, in the State of Lu, from the highest dignitaries down, every one was grasping of power, and all had departed from the true way.

Therefore Confucius accepted no office. He lived in retirement, and arranged the odes, the records, the rites and music. And his pupils grew ever greater in number, while from all sides,

---

[1] *Translators' Note.* Wilhelm translates *pei ch'ên* as *Ministerialen.* The term is applied to the vassals of a subordinate.

from far distant regions, disciples flocked to him.

In the eighth year of Duke Ting (502 B.C.), Kung-Shan Pu-niu felt himself injured by the Chi family. On this account, Yang Hu stirred up rebellion, and wished to dethrone the descendants of the three princely clans (Chi, Mêng, and Shu-Sun), and to put in their place the collateral branches, with which Yang Hu had always stood well. Thereupon he took Baron Huan of Chi captive. But Huan succeeded in escaping through strategy.

In the ninth year of Duke Ting (501 B.C.), Yang Hu fled to Ch'i, because he had not been victorious. In that year Confucius was fifty years old. Kung-Shan Pu-niu, supported by the city of Pi, rebelled against the Chi family. He sent a messenger to summon Confucius. Confucius, who, for a long time, had been following truth, and was experienced in it, had, up to this moment, never had an opportunity for official activity, since no one was in a position to make use of him; so he said: "The founders of the Chou Dynasty, King Wên and King Wu, had their beginnings in Fêng and Hao, and succeeded in founding a kingdom.

Now Pi is, of course, but a small place, but perhaps, even so, much may be possible." He wished to go thither. His disciple, Tze Li, was displeased and prevented Confucius. Confucius said: "It can surely not be chance that he has summoned me! If he understands how to make use of me, perhaps there can be made of him an eastern Chou!" But in the end he did not go after all.[1]

Afterwards Duke Ting appointed Confucius ruler of the middle district (Chung Tu). At the end of a year his neighbours on all sides took him as a model. From the management of Chung Tu, he was advanced to the post of Minister of Public Works. From Minister of Public Works, he was advanced to the post of Minister of Justice.

In the spring of the tenth year of Duke Ting (500 B.C.), Confucius made peace with the State of Ch'i. In the summer, the dignitary, Li Ch'u of Ch'i, said to Duke Ching: "Lu has appointed K'ung Ch'iu to office; his power is growing danger-

[1] Lun Yü, XVII, 5. Compare, on this point, Richard Wilhelm, K'ung-Tse, Leben und Werk, p. 196, note 36.

Translators' Note. "The passage in the Lun Yü seems to be a forged interpolation. The original seat of the Chou Dynasty lay west from Lu."—Legge.

ous." So Ch'i sent an ambassador to Lu, to invite the prince to a friendly gathering. The gathering was to take place in Chia Ku. Duke Ting wished to go thither in a simple chariot, as if to a friendly reunion. Confucius, who was acting Chancellor, said: "I have heard that when one has peaceful business, one must make martial preparations for it, and when one has martial business, one must make peaceful preparations for it. When the princes leave the boundaries of their territories, they must take with them their entire official retinue. So I beg you also to take the Marshal of the Right as well as the Marshal of the Left." Duke Ting said: "Yes," and commanded his Marshals of the Right and of the Left to accompany him. Thus he met with the Prince of Ch'i in Chia Ku.

A terrace was built, to which a threefold staircase led. Then the princes met together, according to the rites, for a meeting. After the princes had bowed, and each had offered the other precedence, they mounted the steps. After the ceremony was concluded, in which each drank to the other, an official of Ch'i advanced and said: "I beg that the music of the four cardinal points be performed."

Duke Ching agreed. Thereupon a crowd appeared, decked in feathers and tails, with feathers and *fu* utensils, spears and lances, swords and shields, and these advanced amid drumbeat and outcry.

Confucius hastened forward, rushing up the steps. On the step before the last, he stood still, raised his sleeve, and said: "Our two princes are here for a friendly meeting. What business has the music of barbarians here? I beg that instructions be given to the officers of the day that the officers of the day scatter these dancers." When they did not depart, the entire company turned its gaze upon Yen Ying and Duke Ching. Duke Ching was inwardly ashamed and caused the musicians to be removed.

After a time, an official of Ch'i appeared and said: "I request that the music of the inner palace be performed." Duke Ching consented, and there appeared jugglers and dwarfs, with their dances. Confucius hastened forward, rushing up the steps. On the step before the last, he stood still and said: "It is a crime meriting death that such fellows dare to disturb the princes. I beg that instructions be given to the officers of the day that the officers of the day carry out the punishments." Then hands and feet flew about separated.[1]

Then Duke Ching was frightened and was aroused, since he knew that he had not behaved quite correctly. After his return, he became very much worried, scolded his officials, and said: "In Lu they uphold their prince after the manner of the sages. You, through your barbaric actions, have brought it about that I have put myself in the wrong with respect to the Prince of Lu. What *can* we do?" An official stepped forward and replied: "If a person of noble character has committed a fault, he excuses himself by means of something actual; if a person of low character has committed

[1] See, in this connection, M. Granet, *Danses et Légendes de la Chine ancienne*, pp. 171-213, and elsewhere. Paris, 1926.

Translators' Note. Chavannes' translation indicates that the limbs of the dwarfs were scattered after they had been killed. The gesture with the sleeve, found in only one of the seven versions of this interview, is an additional ceremonial act by Confucius, to indicate his displeasure at the course of events. Granet notices that in none of the seven versions does Confucius mount to the highest step, which was reserved for princes. The whole incident indicates the triumph of Confucius at this meeting, through strict adherence to ceremonial. This very important meeting at Chia Ku is discussed in great detail and in all its aspects by Granet.

a fault, he excuses himself with words alone. If you have regrets, excuse yourself by means of an actual deed." Thereupon the Prince of Ch'i, in order to make good his fault, returned the territories Yün, Wên Yang, and Kuei Yin, which he had stolen from the State of Lu.

In the summer of the thirteenth year of Ting (497 B.C.), Confucius spoke to Prince Ting: "Among the officials, there must be none who have concealed stores of weapons; among the dignitaries, there must be none who possess cities with walls more than three thousand feet long." Confucius had his disciple, Chung Yu, made steward of the Chi family, with the intention of razing the city walls of the cities of the three clans. Thereupon, the Shu-Sun family first dismantled the walls of Hou. The Chi family was about to raze the walls of Pi, but Kung-Shan Pu-niu and Shu-Sun Ch'ê put themselves at the head of the citizens of Pi and fell upon the Duke of Lu and the three barons. These latter retreated into the fortress of the Chi family, and mounted the tower of Baron Wu. The citizens of Pi attacked them, but could not overcome them. Yet there were some who forced their way into the vicinity of the duke.[1]

Then Confucius commanded Shên Chü-hsü and Yüeh Ch'i to fight against them. The citizens of Pi were conquered, and the state troops pursued them and annihilated them near Ku Mieh. The two insurgents fled to Ch'i, and the walls of Pi were razed.

When they were about to raze the walls of Ch'êng, then Kung-Lien Ch'u-fu said to the Mêng family: "If the walls of Ch'êng are razed, the people of Ch'i will surely soon arrive at the North Gate. And Ch'êng is the fortress of the Mêng family. Without Ch'êng, there will be no Mêng family. I will not let the walls be razed." In the twelfth month, the duke beleaguered the city of Ch'êng, but could not take it.

In the fourteenth year of Duke Ting (496 B.C.), Confucius was fifty-six years old, and received the post of Acting Chancellor, after having been Minister of Justice. He appeared pleased.

[1] The reading "of the tower" is to be preferred to "of the duke."

Translators' Note. The Chia Yü writes *t'ai, tower, platform,* which Chavannes translates *belvédère.*

Then his disciples said: "We have heard that the Sage, when ill-fortune approaches, does not fear, and when good fortune approaches, does not rejoice." Confucius said: "Yes, there is such a saying. But is there not another saying: 'He delights, as a superior man, to condescend in the presence of inferiors?' "

Thereupon he executed, from among the dignitaries of Lu, the trouble-maker, Shao-Chêng Mao.[1]

After Confucius had conducted the government of the state for three months, the sellers of lambs and of suckling pigs no longer falsified their prices, and men and women walked on different sides of the road. Lost objects were not picked up on the streets. Strangers who came from all sides did not need to turn to the officials when they entered the city, for all were received as if they were returning to their own homes.

The people of Ch'i heard of this, and they were afraid, and said: "Confucius is surely carrying on the government in such a fashion that he will

---

[1] This story, which is found neither in the Tso Chüan nor in the Lun Yü, is probably apocryphal.

obtain the hegemony. If he has the hegemony, we shall be the first to be annexed, because our land lies nearest. It is probably wise for us to offer him some territory." Li Ch'u said: "I beg that he first be hindered. If the hindrance is of no avail, there is always time to offer him territory." Thereupon they chose eighty of the most beautiful maidens of Ch'i, dressed them in magnificent garments, and had them practise the dances to the music of K'ang; besides this, they chose thirty sets of four magnificent horses, and sent them as a gift to the Prince of Lu.

The female musicians and the splendid steeds were exhibited in front of the South High Gate of the capital of Lu. Baron Huan of Chi went thither two or three times incognito to see them. He was in favor of accepting them, and talked on the subject to the prince, suggesting that the latter pass that way on a drive. The prince went to behold, and remained the whole day. He neglected the government.

Tze Lu said: "Master, we can go." Confucius said: "Today Lu celebrates the sacrificial feast in the open space before the city. If the dignitaries

are given the customary gift of sacrificial meat,
I can, in spite of what has occurred, remain."

In the end, Baron Huan of Ch'i actually accepted the dancing girls who had been sent as a
present, and for three days all the business of
government ceased. Besides this, the customary
gifts of sacrificial meat were not sent to the dignitaries. Thereupon, Confucius departed.[1]

He passed the night in Tun. The Music-Master,
I, escorted him and said: "Master, no blame at-
taches to you." The Master said: "Shall I sing
you a song?" The song ran as follows:

"O the singing of these women
Has driven me from here.
O the coming of these women
Brings death and ruin!
O Woe! O Wandering!
Even unto life's end!"

The Music-Master, I, returned home. Baron
Huan said: "What, then, did Confucius say?"
The Music-Master, I, reported it to him in ac-

[1] *Translators' Note.* Lun Yü, XVII, 4. Wilhelm's reference
(p. 17) to Lun Yü, XVIII, 4, must be a misprint.

cordance with the truth. Then Baron Huan sighed deeply and said: "The Master ascribes to me the blame for these female slaves!"

Thereupon, Confucius betook himself to the State of Wei, and dwelt in the house of the brother of the wife of his disciple, Tze Lu, whose name was Yen Cho-tsou.

Duke Ling of Wei questioned Confucius as to what salary he had received in Lu. Confucius replied: "I received 60,000 bushels of grain." Thereupon, in Wei, likewise, he was given 60,000 bushels of grain.

After some time, a certain man traduced Confucius to Duke Ling of Wei. Thereupon, Duke Ling commanded Kung-Sun Yü-chia to accompany Confucius wherever he went. Confucius feared that he had fallen into disfavour, so he left Wei after having been there ten months.

He wished to go to Ch'ên and passed through K'uang. Yen Ko drove his chariot. He pointed with his whip to the city and said: "In former times I came into the city through yonder breach." The citizens of K'uang heard this and thought it was Yang Hu of Lu. Now Yang Hu had cruelly

26

dealt with the citizens of K'uang. Therefore the citizens of K'uang detained Confucius. Confucius resembled Yang Hu in form; therefore they took him prisoner. Five days later, Yen Yüan (the favorite disciple of Confucius) followed. The Master said: "I thought you were dead!" Yen Yüan replied: "So long as the Master lives, I may not die." The people of K'uang kept Confucius in ever stricter confinement. His disciples were terrified. But Confucius said: "Since King Wên is no longer alive, this civilization is entrusted to my care! If Heaven wished to destroy this civilization, a mortal in these later days in which I live would not have attained this stage of civilization. But if Heaven does not wish to destroy this civilization, what can the people of K'uang do to me?" [1]

Confucius had one of his followers enter the service of Ning Wu-tze in Wei, and in this manner he was able to escape.

When he left, he passed through P'u. After something more than a month, he returned to Wei, and lived as a guest in the house of Chü Po-yü.

[1] Lun Yü, XI, 22; IX, 5.

Among the wives of Duke Ling was one named Nan Tze. She sent a messenger to say to Confucius: "The lords of all the lands that do not disdain to conclude brotherhood with our prince are always accustomed to see my insignificant self. My insignificance desires to see Confucius also." He wished to refuse, but he was not successful, and was obliged to visit her. The lady sat behind a curtain. Confucius entered the door and bowed in the direction of the North. The lady returned the salutation twice behind the curtain, and as she did so her jade ornaments gave forth a clear sound. Confucius said: "I really did not wish to see her. I have seen her, and she returned my greeting with proper decorum."

Tze Lu was displeased. Then Confucius implored him: "Whatever I have done wrong, Heaven forced me to do, Heaven forced me to do!"

After he had sojourned in Wei for about a month, Prince Ling and his wife took a drive in the same chariot into which Yang Chü mounted as the third member of the party, and the prince let Confucius drive behind in a second chariot.

Thus they drove around on the open market place.

Confucius said: "I have never seen any one who loved spiritual things as much as a pretty face." Since he found this humiliating, he left Wei.[1]

Confucius passed through Ts'ao. In this year Duke Ting of Lu died (495 B.C.). Confucius left Ts'ao and went to Sung. He was practising the rites with his pupils under a great tree. The Marshal of Sung, Huan T'ui, wished to kill Confucius, and therefore had the tree cut down. Confucius departed. His disciples said: "We will go quickly." Then said Confucius: "Heaven has generated the spirit in me; of what avail is Huan T'ui against me?"

Confucius went to Chêng. There he and his pupils lost each other. Confucius stood alone at the East Gate of the suburb. A man of Chêng said to Tze Kung, the disciple of Confucius: "At the East Gate there stands a man whose brow resembles Yao, whose neck resembles Kao Yao, whose shoulders resemble Tze Ch'an; but from the hips down he is three inches shorter than Yü. He stood there as cast down as a dog in a house of

[1] Lun Yü, IX, 17.

mourning." Tze Kung told the story to Confucius. Confucius laughed joyously and said: "The outer form is a secondary matter, but the similarity with a dog in a house of mourning, that fits, that fits."

Confucius went thereupon to Ch'ên, and dwelt in the house of Chêng Tze, the guardian of the wall. After something more than a year, King Fu Ch'ai of Wu attacked the State of Ch'ên, wrested three cities from it, and then withdrew. Baron Yang of Chao attacked the city Chao Ko. The king of Ch'u beleaguered the capital of Ts'ai. The prince of Ts'ai thereupon transferred his seat to Wu. The king of Wu conquered King Kou Chien of Yüeh near Kuai Chi.

A sparrowhawk settled on the palace of Ch'ên and died. An arrow of the wood of the *hou* tree, with a stone head, had pierced it. It was one foot eight inches long. Duke Min of Ch'ên sent a messenger to Chung Ni (Confucius) to ask him about it. Chung Ni said: "The sparrowhawk has come from afar; this is an arrow of the Su Shên.[1] Once, when King Wu had overcome the Shang Dynasty,

[1] The Nü Chên, a Manchurian tribe, are probably meant.

30

he extended his rule to the nine Yi tribes and the hundred Man tribes, and caused them all to appear with the tribute of their country, in order that they might not forget the duties of their station. Then the Su Shên brought arrows of *hou* wood with stone heads. These were one foot eight inches long. The immortal king wished to show his mighty influence, and lent the arrows of the Su Shên to Ta Chi, married her to Duke Hu, the descendant of Shun of Yü, and gave him Ch'ên as a fief.[1] He distributed jade to the blood relatives, in order to secure their allegiance, and he gave to the members of other families tribute gifts from distant regions, in order that they should not forget their submissiveness. Thus he passed on to Ch'ên the arrows of Su Shên." These statements were tested by the old archives, and were found to be actually true.

Confucius dwelt in Ch'ên for three years. It happened that at that time Chin and Ch'u were fighting for the supremacy, and also conquered Ch'ên. Since the State of Wu also fell upon Ch'ên, this state suffered ceaseless plunderings. Con-

---

[1] *Translators' Note.* Ta Chi, eldest daughter of King Wu.

fucius said: "Let me go home, let me go home! My young friends are enthusiastic and do things on a large scale; [1] they make progress, and are not forgetful of their beginnings." Thereupon, Confucius left the State of Ch'ên. He came through P'u. At that very time, Kung-Shu, relying upon P'u, was in a state of rebellion. The people of P'u detained Confucius. Among his disciples was one by the name of Kung-Liang Ju, who joined Confucius with five of his own chariots. He was of ripe age, competent, and full of courageous strength. He said: "When I formerly joined the Master, we met with difficulties in K'uang. Today we again meet with difficulties *here*. That is fate. I will fight and die rather than again see the Master caught in difficulties." He fought so fiercely that the people of P'u were afraid and said: "If you do not go to Wei, we will let you go." Thereupon they swore an agreement with him, and let him depart at the East Gate.

Thereupon, Confucius went to Wei. Tze Kung

[1] Mencius, VII, B. 37.

Translators' Note. Wilhelm's *grosszügig* hardly seems correct, in the light of the Chinese text, since *k'uang chien* rather means *negligent*, or *overhasty*. See p. 40, and note, p. 41.

asked: "Is an oath a thing that one may break?" Confucius replied: "It was an extorted oath; such a one the gods do not hear."

When Duke Ling of Wei heard that Confucius was coming, he rejoiced, and went outside the city as far as the open common to meet him. Duke Ling asked him: "Can P'u be attacked?" Confucius replied: "Yes." Duke Ling said: "My dignitaries are of the opinion that it is not possible. Now P'u is the place where Wei must offer resistance to the States of Chin and Ch'u. If now we attack it from Wei, is not that, after all, not feasible?"

Confucius said: "The men there are true unto death; the women think only of guarding the river in the west; at most, there will be four or five against whom we must fight."

Duke Ling said: "Good!" But nevertheless he did not attack P'u. Duke Ling had grown old, and he no longer regarded the government as important; therefore he did not make use of the counsels of Confucius. Confucius sighed and said: "If some one would make use of me, something would be seen in a year and a day; in three years, all would surely be settled." Thereupon, Confucius departed.[1]

Pi Hsi was governor of Chung Mou. When Baron Chien of Chou attacked the families of Fan and Chung Hang, he also fought Chung Mou. Pi Hsi rebelled. He sent a messenger to summon Confucius. Confucius wished to go. Tze Lu said: "I have heard the Master say that if any one is himself guilty of wrongdoing the Sage will not associate with him. Now Pi Hsi himself has rebelled in Chung Mou, and yet you wish to go there; how do you reconcile that?" Confucius replied: "Yes, there is such a saying. But is there not another saying: 'That which is hard can be ground without becoming thin'? Is there not yet another saying: 'That which is white can be dipped in a thick and muddy liquid without becoming black'? Am I, then, perhaps a gourd that is hung up without being eaten?"[2]

[1] Lun Yü, XIII, 10.

[2] Lun Yü, XVII, 7.

Translators' Note. The end of this paragraph is extremely difficult. Both Legge and Chavannes agree in the interpretation that the sage can touch pitch and not be defiled. Wilhelm is less definite, but the Chinese seems clearly to point to this.

The Chinese ideogram which Wilhelm translates as *der Edle,*

Confucius struck the musical stone. A man carrying a basket was passing the door, and he said: "The one who strikes the musical stone is very serious. But why be so obstinate? If no one knows us, let us give it up and have done with it!" [1]

Confucius learned from the Music-Master, Hsiang Tze, to play the zither. For ten days, Confucius made no progress. The Music-Master, Hsiang Tze, said: "We will try something else." Confucius said: "I have practised the melody, but I have not yet acquired the rhythm." After a time, the Music-Master said: "Now that you have practised the rhythm, we will proceed." Confucius said: "I have not yet caught the mood." After a

der höhere Mensch, or der Weise, and Chavannes as le sage, is translated by Legge as the superior man. It is the chün tze, which also has the idea of gentleman. The term is one of the most important in the Confucian canon. Its opposite, hsiao jen, literally means the little man. Legge translates, the mean man; Wilhelm, der Gemeine (the common man), but the word hsiao here has definitely qualitative connotations. In general, we have rendered Wilhelm's der Edle by the Sage, his der hohere Mensch by the superior man, his der Weise by the Philosopher. More latitude seemed necessary in rendering der Gemeine.

[1] Lun Yü, XIV, 42.

while, the Music-Master spoke again: "Now that you have practised the mood, we will proceed." Confucius said: "I have not yet ascertained what kind of man composed the music." After a time the Music-Master said: "You are so serious and sunk in thought. You are so cheerful, so full of high hopes, and of an open mood." Confucius said: "Now I know who he is. Dark and black, tall and large. His eyes are those of a ram looking into the distance; his mind is that of a king of the four quarters of the earth. If it was not King Wên, who else could have composed anything like this?" Then the Music-Master, Hsiang Tze, arose from his mat, bowed twice, and said: "According to the tradition of the Music-Masters, it is actually reputed to be a melody by King Wên."

Since Confucius found no use for his services in Wei, he was about to turn west, in order to see Baron Chien of Chao. But when he came to the Yellow River, he heard that Fu Ming-tu and Shun Hua had been killed. He stepped to the river, and sighing said: "How beautiful is the water, how powerful its current! That I shall not cross it,

36

that is fate!" Tze Kung hastened to him and asked: "May I inquire what that signifies?" Confucius replied: "Fu Ming-tu and Shun Hua were the most competent dignitaries of the State of Chin. Before Baron Chien of Chao had attained his goal, he made use of the two men to carry on the government. I have heard that where people cut open mother animals, in order to kill the unborn offspring, the *Ch'i lin* does not come to the pasture.[1] Where the ponds are drained, in order to catch the fish on dry land, the dragons do not bring into harmony the powers of darkness and of light. Where the nests are destroyed, in order to take out the eggs, thither the phoenixes do not come flying. Why is this? All that is noble avoids the suffering of its own kind. If even birds and beasts know how to restrain themselves in the face of injustice, how should I do otherwise."

Thereupon he turned about, and rested in the

[1] *Translators' Note.* The *ch'i lin* is a fabulous animal, which is said to have appeared first in 2600 B.C., in the grounds of the emperor Huang Ti. One of these creatures is said to have appeared to the mother of Confucius before his birth, and tradition has it that it appears when sages are born. It is the so-called *fo dog*, so often found in the curio shops. See p. 13 and note; p. 49 and note; p. 62 and note, for fabulous animals.

market town of Tsou. He composed the song of Tsou, in order to give expression to his grief. Thereupon he returned to Wei, and dwelt in the house of Chü Po-yü.

One day Duke Ling interrogated Confucius concerning battle array. Confucius said: "Concerning the arrangement of sacrificial vessels, I am informed; concerning the arrangement of armies, I have as yet learned nothing." On the following day, Duke Ling had a conversation with Confucius. Then Duke Ling saw a wild goose. He looked up at it, and seemed to be paying no attention to Confucius. Thereupon, Confucius took his departure. He went again to Ch'ên.[1]

In the summer of the year 493 B.C., Duke Ling died. His grandson, Chao, succeeded to the throne.[2] He was Duke Ch'u of Wei.

In the sixth month, Ch'ao Yang gave the crown prince, K'uai Wai, a fief in Ch'i. Yang Hu caused

[1] Lun Yü, XV, 1.

[2] *Translators' Note.* The ideogram which Chavannes and Wilhelm here transliterate as *Chao* is, in the 1742 edition of the Historical Annals, and in at least two others (kindly collated for us by Mr. Yen, of the Columbia University Library), usually rendered Ch'ê or possibly Chê. Giles Dictionary, No. 581.

the crown prince to put on mourning garb. Eight men, dressed in mourning, came, apparently from Wei. He went weeping to meet them. Thereupon, he settled in the city.

In the winter, the Prince of Ts'ai changed his capital city to Chou Lai. This was the third year of Duke Ai of Lu. Confucius was then sixty years old.

The State of Ch'i helped the State of Wei to beleaguer the city of Ch'i, because the crown prince, K'uai Wai, dwelt there.[1]

In the summer, the ancestral temples of the Dukes Huan and Li, of Lu, burned down. Nan-Kung Ching-shu fought the fire. Confucius was in Ch'ên, and heard of this. Then he said: "Misfortune has, of a certainty, befallen the temples of Dukes Huan and Li!" And in truth that had been the case.

In the autumn, Baron Huan of Chi fell ill. He caused himself to be driven out in a chariot, in order once more to view the city walls. Sighing, he said: "There was a time when this state almost

[1] *Translators' Note.* In Chinese, two entirely different ideograms are used for *Ch'i*, the State, and *Ch'i*, the city.

reached a peak of prosperity. Because I was at fault with respect to Confucius, therefore my state did not reach a peak of prosperity." Then he turned to his heir, Baron K'ang, and said: "When I die, you will surely become Chancellor in Lu. When you are Chancellor, you must summon Chung Ni." Some days later, Baron Huan died, and Baron K'ang was installed in his place. After the burial, he wished to summon Chung Ni (Confucius). But Kung Chih-yü said: "Once our sainted lord appointed him, but did not carry the affair to a conclusion: thus he brought down upon himself the laughter of the princes. Now, if you appoint him again, and once more cannot carry on to the end, you will become the mock of the princes." Baron K'ang said: "Whom, then, can I summon?" But Kung Chih-yü replied: "You must call Jan Ch'iu to office." So he sent a messenger to summon Jan Ch'iu. As Jan Ch'iu was departing, Confucius said: "When Jan Ch'iu is summoned to Lu, it is not done for small purposes, but for great purposes." On this day, Confucius said: "I want to go home, I want to go home! My young pupils are enthusiastic and do things on a large scale. They are skilled in all the fine arts. But I do not know how they 'restrict and shape themselves.' " [1]

Tze Kung knew that Confucius was thinking of returning home. He accompanied Jan Ch'iu, and warned him, as follows: "When you enter upon your official duties, see to it that Confucius is summoned." Thereupon, Jan Ch'iu departed.

In the following year (491 B.C.), Confucius betook himself from Ch'en to Ts'ai. Duke Chao of Ts'ai wished to go to the State of Wu, since the King of Wu had summoned him. Since Duke Chao had previously deceived his ministers when he changed his capital to Chou Lai, the dignitaries were afraid, when he wished to depart, that he would once more change the position of his capital city. Therefore Kung-Sun P'ien shot him with an arrow. The State of Ch'u invaded Ts'ai. In the autumn, Duke Ching of Ch'i died.

[1] Lun Yü, V, 21. That this phrase has already been mentioned once in the version of Mencius is certainly based on an error. It is a question of the same affair.

Translators' Note. The ideogram *ts'ai*, which Wilhelm translates by *zurechtschneiden*, is translated by Legge as above, in single quotation marks. *Ts'ai* may mean either to *cut* (as garments), or to *regulate*.

In the following year (489 B.C.), Confucius went from Ts'ai to Shê. The Duke of Shê asked concerning the best manner of governing. Confucius replied: "Governing consists in enticing those from a distance, and in retaining those who are near." [1]

On the next day the Duke of Shê questioned Tze Lu about Confucius. Confucius heard this and said: "Yu, why did you not reply: he is a man who learns truth without growing weary, who instructs mankind without becoming disgusted, who is so zealous that he forgets his food, who is so joyous that he forgets all care, and so does not observe the gradual approach of old age." [2]

Then Confucius left Shê, and returned to Ts'ai. Ch'ang Chü and Chieh Ni were weeding and hoeing. Confucius marked that they were philosophers under the surface. [3] He sent Tze Lu to ask about the ford. Ch'ang Chü said: "Who is he who is

[1] Lun Yü, XIII, 16.

Translators' Note. Legge's translation: "Good government obtains when those who are near are made happy and when those who are far off are attracted."

[2] Lun Yü, VII, 18.

[3] Lun Yü, XVIII, 6.

halting his chariot there?" Tze Lu replied: "It is K'ung Ch'iu." The other said: "Is it K'ung Ch'iu of Lu?" Tze Lu answered: "Yes." Ch'ang Chü said: "Then, of course he knows the ford." Thereupon, Chieh Ni said to Tze Lu: "And who are you?" He replied: "I am Chung Yu." [1] The other asked: "Are you a disciple of Confucius?" He answered: "Yes." Chieh Ni said: "Such a deluge prevails over the whole world, and who can change it? Would it not be better, instead of following a master who withdraws from individual men, to follow one who withdraws from the world?" With that, he continued to dig, and did not stop again.

Tze Lu reported this to Confucius. Confucius was cast down and said: "I really cannot live with birds and beasts. If order prevailed on earth, I should, of course, need to change nothing!"

On another day, Tze Lu was under way, and met an old man who was carrying a basket on his shoulder. He said to him: "Have you seen the Master?" The old man replied: "Your four limbs are not fit for work. You cannot distinguish between the five kinds of grain. Who is your

---

[1] The personal name of Tze Lu.

Master?" With that, he stuck his staff into the ground, and began to weed.[1]

Tze Lu reported this to Confucius, who said: "He is a hermit." Tze Lu returned to that spot, but the old man had gone.

Three years after Confucius had settled in Ts'ai (489 B.C.), Wu attacked the State of Ch'ên, and Ch'u, coming to the help of Ch'ên, camped in Ch'êng Fu. The king of Ch'u heard that Confucius was between Ch'ên and Ts'ai, so he sent a messenger with an invitation to Confucius. Confucius was about to go thither, to return thanks for the invitation. Then the dignitaries of Ch'ên and Ts'ai took counsel among themselves and said: "Confucius is a Sage; whatever criticism he had to offer concerns the faults of the feudal princes. Now he has been living for a long time in the neighbourhood of Ch'ên and Ts'ai. What we have done here is not in accordance with the views of Chung Ni. Ch'u is a large state, and is now extending an invitation to Confucius. If Confucius obtains influence in Ch'u, the conditions will become dangerous for the leading dignitaries of

[1] Lun Yü, XVIII, 7.

44

Ch'ên and Ts'ai. Thereupon, they together sent out servants, who surrounded Confucius in the field, so that he could not proceed. His provisions gave out, and his disciples were so weak that they could no longer stand up. But Confucius continued to expound and recite the sacred writings, and to play and sing. Tze Lu was displeased, and, stepping before Confucius, said: "Has the Sage also such want?" Confucius answered: "The superior man remains firm in want, but when want overtakes the inferior man he gives way to license."[1]

Tze Kung was excited. Confucius said: "Tzu, you probably think that I have learned much, and now know it." Tze Kung replied: "Yes. Is that not true?" Confucius said: "No; I have one thing to permeate everything."[2]

Confucius, knowing that the disciples murmured in their hearts, called Tze Lu to him and asked him: "In the Book of Odes it is written: 'We are neither rhinoceroses nor tigers, that we could stay in this wilderness.' Is my teaching per-

[1] Lun Yü, XV, 1.

[2] Lun Yü, XV, 2.

Translators' Note. Legge translates: "I seek a unity all-pervading."

haps false? Why does this want befall us?" Tze
Lu answered: "I suppose that I have not yet attained true goodness, and that therefore people
do not trust me. I suppose that I have not yet
attained true wisdom, and that therefore people
will not yet do what I say." Confucius said: "Do
you really think so? If, however, good men were
invariably to gain confidence, how would the lot
of a Po I and a Shu Ch'i have been possible? If
the words of the Philosophers invariably found
obedience, how could there have been a Prince
Pi Kan?"

Tze Lu went out. Tze Kung came in, and
stepped before Confucius. The latter said: "Tzu,
in the Book of Odes it is written: 'We are neither
rhinoceroses nor tigers, that we could stay in this
wilderness.' Is my teaching perhaps false? Why
does this want befall us?" Tze Kung answered:
"The Master's teaching is so overpowering that
no one on earth can bear it. You must, I think,
bring it a little lower." Confucius said: "Tzu, a
good husbandman can sow, but he cannot make
the harvest. A good workman can be clever, but
he cannot always meet people's taste. The Sage

may cultivate his doctrines, may arrange them and simplify them, may co-ordinate them and judge them, but he cannot bring it to pass that they be accepted. If you now think that one needs only to cultivate one's doctrines, and if you strive only to have them accepted, then, Tzu, your vision is not directed afar."

Tze Kung went out. Yen Hui came in, and stepped before Confucius. The latter said: "In the Book of Odes it is written: 'We are neither rhinoceroses nor tigers that we could stay in this wilderness.' How is it that this want befalls us?" Yen Hui answered: "Your teaching, Master, is very great; therefore the world cannot comprehend it. Nevertheless, continue, Master, to act according to it. What matters it that it is not comprehended? In the very fact that he is not understood, the Sage is recognized. If we do not cultivate our doctrines, that is our error. But if we painstakingly cultivate our doctrines, and these doctrines are not accepted, that is the fault of the rulers of the land. What matters it that the doctrine is not understood? In the very fact that he is not understood, the Sage is recognized."

47

Confucius rejoiced and smiled. He said: "Son of the house of Yen, if you had great riches, I should wish to be your overseer."

Thereupon, Confucius sent Tze Kung to Ch'u. King Chao of Ch'u sent out soldiers to meet Confucius. So Confucius and his disciples succeeded in making their escape. King Chao had the intention of giving Confucius in fief a territory of 700 square miles. Then Minister Tze Hsi of Ch'u said: "Is there among the ambassadors whom you, O King, send to the princes any who is the equal of Tze Kung?" The King answered: "No." "Is there among Your Majesty's counsellors any who is the equal of Yen Hui?" The king answered: "No." "Is there among Your Majesty's generals any who is the equal of Tze Lu?" The king answered: "No." "Is there among Your Majesty's officials any who is the equal of Tsai Yü?" The king answered: "No." "And now the ancestor of Ch'u was given by the House of Chou a fief of fifty miles as Baron or Viscount. But K'ung Ch'iu continues the methods of the three dynasties, and makes glorious the work of the Dukes of Chou and Shao. If Your Majesty should appoint him, how then would it be possible for the kingdom of Ch'u to extend itself, proud and prosperous, from generation to generation, over thousands of square miles? King Wên in Fêng and King Wu in Hao were princes with a possession of but a hundred miles, and they finally attained world rule. If now K'ung Ch'iu (Confucius) receives land in fief upon which he can rely, and has such excellent disciples to help him, that will not redound to the good fortune of Ch'u." Thereupon, King Chao relinquished the idea of giving land in fief to Confucius. In the autumn of the year (489 B.C.), King Chao of Ch'u died in Ch'eng Fu.

Chieh Yü, the court fool of Ch'u, passed Confucius, singing. He sang:

"O bird Fêng, O bird Fêng!
How greatly did thy splendour dim!
But what is done is done;
Yet in the future be on guard!
Give o'er, give o'er, thy idle striving!
He who today will serve the state
But plunges into perils." [1]

[1] Lun Yü, XVIII, 5.

Translators' Note. The *fêng* is the fabulous phoenix, pre-

The Master dismounted and desired speech with the jester. But the fool fled, so that Confucius could not speak with him.

Thereupon, Confucius left Ch'u and returned to Wei. In this year Confucius was sixty-three years old (489 B.C.). It was the sixth year of Duke Ai, of Lu.

In the following year (488 B.C.), Wu held a conference with Lu in Tsêng. Wu demanded a hecatomb. Chancellor P'i demanded it of Baron K'ang of Chi. Baron K'ang had Tze Kung accompany him, and thus the matter could be avoided.

Confucius said: "The governments of Lu and of Wei are brothers." [1]

At that time, the father of Chê, the Prince of Wei, could not ascend the throne, and tarried outside his domains. The various princes had already frequently made representations on this account. But among the disciples of Confucius many were in the service of Wei. The Prince of Wei wished to obtain Confucius to conduct the government.

eminent among birds. Its appearance was regarded as a symbol of approval of a peaceful reign and a successful ruler.

[1] Lun Yü, XIII, 7.

Tze Lu said: "The Prince of Wei expects you to conduct the government for him. What do you consider the most urgent matter?" Confucius answered: "Under all the circumstances, the rectification of the names." Tze Lu said: "Ought that to be the question? Master, you have erred greatly; what shall their rectification avail?" Confucius replied: "How untutored you are, Yu! If the names are not correct, the judgments are not clear. If the judgments are not clear, the works are not accomplished. If the works are not accomplished, then rites and music do not flourish. If rites and music do not flourish, punishments are not equitable. If the punishments are not just, then the people are at a complete loss. The Sage always gives such a turn to his actions that they can be called by their right names (idea) and always gives such a turn to his judgments that they can be carried out. The Sage permits nothing inexact in his words." [1]

In the following year (484 B.C.), Jan Ch'iu was in command of the army of the Chi family, and fought against Ch'i at Lang, and conquered

[1] *Translators' Note.* Cf. pp. 148 ff. and Translators' Note, p. 151.

it. Baron K'ang of Chi said: "Have you attained your military skill by learning it or is it naturally yours?" Jan Ch'iu answered: "I have learned it of Confucius." Baron K'ang of Chi asked: "What sort of man is Confucius?" Jan Ch'iu replied: "If one makes use of him, one will reap fame. If one asks the people about him, or lets the gods and spirits express themselves concerning him, no one of them will be dissatisfied. He strives to attain the highest that is possible on the path of virtue.[1] If you assign him a territory of 1,000 miles, he will not regard that as gain!" Baron K'ang said: "I should like to summon him. Can that be done?" Jan Ch'iu replied: "If you wish to summon him, you must not let him be circumvented by inferior people; then it can be done."

In Wei, K'ung Wen-tze wished to attack T'ai Shu, and he asked Chung Ni (Confucius) for counsel. Chung Ni refused, as he understood nothing of the matter. He withdrew, caused the horses to be put to his chariot, and departed. He

[1] *Translators' Note.* What Wilhelm translates *auf diesem Weg das Höchste* is actually a rendition of the so variously translated *tao*, which always seems to have a moral connotation. Chavannes thus interprets it.

said: "The bird can seek a tree for himself, but a tree cannot seek a bird." Wên Tze wished to detain him, but Baron K'ang of Chi sent the honorable Hua, the honorable Pin, and the honorable Lin to receive him with gifts of silk. Then Confucius returned to Lu.

Confucius had been away from Lu for fourteen years at the time when he returned to Lu.

Duke Ai questioned him regarding the government. Confucius replied: "The government consists in the correct choice of officials."

Baron K'ang of Chi asked him about the government. Confucius replied: "One must elevate the just men, so that they exert pressure upon the crooked men; in this way the crooked will become straight." [1]

Baron K'ang was distressed concerning the great number of thefts. Confucius said: "If you did not countenance thefts, the people would not steal, even though you rewarded them for it." [2]

---

[1] Lun Yü, XII, 22.
[2] *Ibid.*, 18.

But finally it turned out that they could not make use of Confucius in Lu. And neither did Confucius strive for official position.

In the days of Confucius, the House of Chou had degenerated, the rites and music had fallen into decay, songs and records showed lacunae. Therefore Confucius followed the traces of the rites of the three dynasties, arranged the traditional material of the records, beginning from above, with the events under the rulers of T'ang (Yao) and of Yü (Shun), and going down to Duke Mu of Ch'in. He arranged and grouped the events in their reigns.

Confucius said: "Concerning the rites of the Hsia Dynasty, I might speak; but the State of Chi is not in a position to furnish the necessary corroborative data. Concerning the rites of the Yin Dynasty, I might speak; but the State of Sung is not in a position to furnish the necessary corroborative data. If they were in such a position, I could verify everything.[1] When one considers what the Dynasties of Yin and Hsia have subtracted from the existing rites, and what they have

[1] Lun Yü, III, 9.

54

added to them, one knows the future for a hundred generations to come.[1] Equally strong in form and content, and of a fine completeness, the Chou Dynasty looks back upon its predecessors. Of a truth, I shall hold to the Chou Dynasty."

Therefore the transmission of the records and the determination of the rites come to us through Confucius.

Confucius spoke to the Chief Music-Master: "One can know how music must be played. At the beginning of the piece, all the parts sound together; the continuation must bring out the individual themes in a harmonious manner, and without a break, to the conclusion. When I returned to Lu from Wei, the music was reformed. The art songs and the praise songs all attained their proper place." [2]

In olden times, there were over 3,000 songs. Confucius, for his part, eliminated the repetitions, and included those songs which were of value for morals and justice. Beginning from above with

---

[1] *Translators' Note.* Lun Yü, II, XXIII, 2. Wilhelm's reference to Lun Yü, IX, 14, must be a misprint.

[2] Lun Yü, III, 23; IX, 14.

Hsieh and Hou Tze, in the middle he transcribed the songs from the period of the efflorescence of Yin and Chou, proceeding down to the defective periods of King Yu and King Li. He began with the love songs; therefore he put the full tones of the Kuan Chü song at the beginning of the folk songs, the ode Lu-Ming at the beginning of the minor art songs, the ode Wên-Wang at the beginning of the major art songs, and the ode Ch'ing Miao at the beginning of the praise songs. All the three hundred and five pieces Confucius accompanied with the strings, and he sang them in order to attain agreement with the music of Shao, Wu, Ya, and Sung. From that point on, one could survey the rites and music, in order thus to prepare the way for the kingdom, and to complete the six arts.

Confucius had, in his later years, a great love for the Book of Changes; for its arrangement, as well as for its explanations, additions, pictures, treatises, and commentaries. He read so much in the Book of Changes that he three times wore out the leather thong which held the book together. He said: "If a few more years are granted me, I shall be an adept with respect to the 'Changes.' " [1]

Confucius gave instruction to about 3,000 pupils in the odes, records, rites, and music. Among these pupils there were seventy-two who were personally the masters of all six arts. Pupils like Yen, Cho, and Tsou, who had enjoyed a considerable amount of his instruction, were very numerous.

Confucius gave instruction in four subjects: Literature, Conduct, Conscientiousness, and Loyalty. He was free from four things: he had "no foregone conclusions, no arbitrary predeterminations, no obstinacy, and no egoism." The matters in which he exercised the greatest caution were the periods of fasting, of warfare, of illness. The Master seldom spoke of fortune, of fate, of "perfect virtue." [2]

[1] Lun Yü, VII, 16.

Translators' Note. Legge's translation: "The Master said: 'If some years were added to my life, I would give fifty to the study of the Yi [Changes], and then I might be without great faults.' "

[2] Lun Yü, IX, 4; VII, 12; IX, 1.

Translators' Note. The quotation marks in the above paragraph indicate Legge's renderings. The first Lun Yü reference is interesting. In Legge's translation it runs: "The Master said: 'From the man bringing his bundle of dried flesh for my teaching upwards, I have never refused instruction to any one.' "

He gave no help to him who was not zealous. If he presented one corner of a subject as an example, and the pupil could not transfer what he had learned to the other three corners, Confucius did not repeat.[1]

In everyday life, Confucius was altogether modest, as though he were not able to speak. In the ancestral temple and at court, he was eloquent, yet his speeches were always cautious. At court, he conversed with the upper dignitaries in exact and definite terms; with the lower dignitaries he was free and open. Whenever he entered in at the duke's door, he walked as though bowed over, with quick steps; he approached as if on wings. Whenever the Prince commanded his presence at a reception of guests, his appearance was serious. Whenever a command of the Prince summoned him, he left his house without waiting for the horses to be put to his chariot.[2]

If fish were no longer fresh, or if the meat was tainted, or not cut in the proper manner, he did not eat it.[3]

[1] Lun Yü, VII, 8.   [3] Lun Yü, X, 8.
[2] Lun Yü, X, 1, 2, 3, 13.

If the mat did not lie straight, he did not seat himself. When he sat at food by one in mourning, he did not eat his fill. When, on any day, he had wept, on that day he sang no more. When he saw a man who was fasting, or who was in mourning or blind, even if it were but a boy, he became serious.[1]

He said, "When three of us are together, there is certainly a master for me among them."[2]

"That virtue is not cultivated, that knowledge is not made clear, that people hear of duty and do not practise it, that people have evil in themselves and do nothing to improve: those are things that make me sad."[3]

When any one sang and did it well, Confucius caused him to repeat it, and then he accompanied him.[4]

[1] Lun Yü, X, 9; VII, 9; IX, 9; X, 16.

Translators' Note. The last reference to the Lun Yü contains a slight variant: for Wilhelm's *wenn es auch nur ein Knabe war,* the reading is, *though he (Confucius) might be informally dressed.*

[2] Lun Yü, VII, 21.

[3] *Ibid.,* 3.

[4] *Ibid.,* 31.

Translators' Note. Wilhelm has *begleitete;* the Chinese ideogram means to *sing in unison with,* or *to sing the second part.*

Things of which the Master did not speak were misused powers and unnatural demons.[1]

Tze Kung said: "The Master's words concerning art and culture are to be heard, but when the Master speaks concerning the way of Heaven or concerning natural talents, these things are not so easily to be heard." [2]

Yen Yüan said with a sigh: "The more I look up, the higher it rises before me; the more I strive to penetrate, the more impenetrable does it become for me. I look forward, then it is suddenly behind me; but the Master knows how to arrange everything in order, and he is skilled in leading men on.[3] He has enlarged my vision through art, and has taught me the restraints of propriety. If I were to wish to give over studying his doctrines, I

---

[1] Lun Yü, VII, 20.

Translators' Note. The Chinese has but four ideograms: *kuai, li, lüan, shên.* The usual translation makes each of these ideograms a noun: *extraordinary things, strength, confusion, spiritual beings.* Wilhelm's translation is quite original in making the first and third ideograms adjectives modifying the second and fourth: *verkehrte Kräfte und widernatürliche Dämonen.*

[2] Lun Yü, V, 12.

Translators' Note. This is one of the most perplexing sections in the Lun Yü.

[3] Lun Yü, IX, 10.

could not. But when I exhaust all my powers, he suddenly rises in sheer grandeur before me, and even if I try to follow him, I find no way to do it."

A youth from the region of Ta Hsiang once said: "Confucius is great, his learning is extensive, but he has not made a name for himself through anything in particular." The Master heard this and said: "What shall I practise—charioteering or archery? I will practise charioteering." [1]

Lao said: "The Master was accustomed to say: 'I was not in office: therefore I have many skills.'" [2]

In the spring of the fourteenth year of Duke Ai of Lu (481 B.C.), there was a hunt in the great wilderness. The charioteer of the chariot of the Shu-Sun family, whose name was Ch'u Shang, slew a beast. He considered it an omen of evil. Chung Ni (Confucius) saw this and said: "It is a *ch'i lin*." So they took it with them.

Confucius said: "The Yellow River sends no

[1] Lun Yü, IX, 2.
[2] *Ibid.*, 6.

plan, the River Lo sends no record. I am done for!"[1]

Yen Yüan died, and Confucius said: "Heaven is destroying me."[2]

When they were hunting in the west, and a *ch'i lin* appeared, Confucius said: "My career is at an end."

He drew a deep sigh and said: "Alas, no one knows me!" Tze Kung said: "What is the meaning of your saying that no one knows you, Master?" The Master said: "I do not murmur against Heaven, I do not grumble against man. I pursue my studies here on earth, and am in touch with heaven above. It is Heaven that knows me![3]

"Those who did not lower their standards and did not shut their eyes to corruption were perhaps Po I and Shu Ch'i. Concerning Hui of Liu Hsia and Shao Lien it must be said that they lowered their standards and shut their eyes to corruption.

[1] Lun Yü, IX, 8.

Translators' Note. The text of the Lun Yü is here quite different. Where Sse-Ma has the Yellow River, the Chinese text of the Lun Yü has the ideogram for *phoenix.*

[2] Lun Yü, XI, 8.

[3] Lun Yü, XIV, 37.

Of Yü Chung and I Yi it may be said that they dwelt in seclusion and refrained from speaking.[1] In their conduct, they conformed to purity, and in their retirement they maintained the balance of conduct. I am different from these: for me there is no may and no must." The Master continued: "No! No! The Sage suffers because he must leave the world without his name being mentioned! My path is not travelled. Through what shall I be known to posterity?"[2] Thereupon, in connection with the data of the Annalists, he composed the Spring and Autumn Annals. Beginning with Duke Yin (722-712 B.C.) and continuing the recording of events down to the fourteenth year of Duke Ai (481 B.C.), he treated the history of twelve dukes, basing his work on Lu, and taking the point of view of Chou; herein he depicted the history of all three dynasties. The style of the text was conservative, but the secret meaning was very far-reaching. Thus the Princes of Wu and Ch'u called themselves "Kings," but this is criticized in the Spring and Autumn Annals by con-

[1] *Translators' Note.* Cf. Lun Yü, XVIII, 8.
[2] Lun Yü, XV, 19.

sistently calling them "Barons." At the assembly
of princes at Chien T'u, in the year 632 B.C., they
had in fact simply fetched the Son of Heaven, but
in the Spring and Autumn Annals this expression is avoided, and the reading is: "The Son of
Heaven was hunting north of the Yellow River."
By the application of this method, the clue is found
for the meaning according to which the events in
each generation are to be criticized or are to be
passed over in silence. If, later on, a king comes,
and comprehends and interprets this meaning, and
carries out the true significance of the Spring and
Autumn Annals in his own rule, then rebellious
officials and robber sons will become afraid. As
long as Confucius was in office, he acted practically the same as other people with respect to
the manner in which he settled law-suits and pronounced judgments, and he made no exceptions.
But when he wrote the Spring and Autumn Annals, then he set down what had to be set down,
and expunged what was to be expunged, so that
Tze Hsia and his pupils could not find a word to
add to his praise. When he delivered the Spring
and Autumn Annals to his disciples, Confucius

said: "If any one recognizes my greatness in future generations, it will be because of the Spring and Autumn Annals. If any one condemns me in future generations, it will likewise be because of the Spring and Autumn Annals."[1]

In the following year, Tze Lu died in Wei (480 B.C.).

Confucius was ill. Tze Kung asked permission to visit him. Then Confucius walked back and forth in the courtyard, supporting himself on his staff, and said: "Tzu, why are you so late?" Then Confucius sighed and sang:

> "The Sacred Mountain caves in,
> The roof beam breaks,
> The Sage will vanish."[2]

Then he shed tears and said to Tze Kung: "For a long time the world has been unregulated; no one understood how to follow me. The people of Hsia placed the coffin upon the east steps, the people of Chou placed it on the west steps, the people of Yin placed it between the two pillars. Last night

[1] Mencius, III, Part II, Chap. 9, § 8.
[2] *Translators' Note.* The Sacred Mountain is T'ai Shan in Shantung.

I dreamed that I was sitting before the sacrificial offerings between the two pillars. Does that mean that I am a man of Yin?" Seven days later, Confucius died. Confucius had attained an age of seventy-three years, when he died, in the fourth month of the sixteenth year of Duke Ai of Lu (479 B.C.).

Duke Ai composed a song of mourning for Confucius: "Merciful Heaven, thou hast had no compassion upon me, in that thou hast not left me the one aged man fitted to protect me, the Unique One, during the period of my rule. Full of mourning am I in my pain! O woe! Father Ni! Now I no longer have any one who could serve me as a model."

Tze Kung said: "The Prince will surely not die a peaceful death in his land of Lu! The Master always said: 'If one does not observe the rites, one is besotted; if one misses the correct names, one goes astray. If one misses obtaining people's good will, one is besotted; if one misses the position that is due to him, one goes astray. If no one has made inquiry for a person while he lived, that is not according to decorum; if a territorial prince calls himself by the designation of the Great King, the 'Unique One,' that is not the correct name."

Confucius was buried north of the city, on the bank of the River Szu.

All the disciples mourned him for three years. When the three years of the mourning of the heart were over,[1] then they separated and went their ways, and once more each one wept bitter tears wrung from his heart. Some there were who remained even longer. Tze Kung alone built himself a hut by the grave mound. He remained, in all, six years before he departed. There were over a hundred families of the disciples of Confucius and of the people of Lu who went thither and built houses by the grave. So they called the place the Hamlet of Confucius. In Lu, the custom was handed down from generation to generation to offer sacrifices at the grave of Confucius at fixed times of the year. And the scholars also practised the rites of a communal banquet and held a great archery contest at the grave of Confucius. The burial place of Confucius is one hundred acres in

[1] That is, without mourning garb, which, according to custom, was only worn after the death of a father.

extent. The Hall [1] in which the pupils of Confucius dwelt was later turned into a temple in which the clothes, hats, lute, chariots, and books of Confucius were preserved. All of this was kept for over two hundred years, until the Han period. When the first emperor of the Han Dynasty came through Lu, he offered a great sacrifice to Confucius. When princes, dignitaries, and ministers come, they always first visit the temple, before they go about their business.

Confucius begat Li, whose appellation was Po-yü. Po-yü died before his father, at the age of fifty. Po-yü begat Chi, whose appellation was Tze-ssu. Tze-ssu lived to be sixty-two years old. He was at one time in danger in Sung. Tze-ssu wrote the Doctrine of the Mean. Tze-ssu begat Po, with the appellation Tze-shang. He lived to be forty-seven years old. Tze-shang begat Ch'iu, with the appellation Tze-chia. He lived to be forty-five years old. Tze-chia begat Chi, with the appellation

---

[1] Cf. the text correction of Chavannes in his translation, Vol. V, p. 429.

Translators' Note. Chavannes accepts the text correction proposed by the commentator Fang Pao, which changes the order of the Chinese ideograms.

Tze-ching. He lived to be forty-six years old. Tze-ching begat Ch'üan, with the appellation Tze-kao. He lived to be fifty-one years old. Tze-kao begat Tze-shên. He lived to be fifty-seven years old. He was Minister in Wei.

Tze-shên begat Fu. He lived to be fifty-seven years old. He was the archaeologist of King Ch'ên Shê and died in Ch'ên. The younger brother of Fu, by name, Tze-hsiang, lived fifty-seven years. He was the archaeologist of the Emperor Hsiao Hui (194-188 B.C.), and was appointed governor of Ch'ang Sha. He was nine feet six inches tall.

Tze-hsiang begat Chung. He lived to be fifty-seven years old. Chung begat Wu, Wu begat Yen-nien and An-kuo. An-kuo was the archaeologist of the present emperor. He attained to the rank of Governor of Lin Huai. He died before his time.

An-kuo begat Ang. Ang begat Huan.

The Chief Historian says: "In the Book of Odes it is written:

'The high mountain, he looked toward it;
The distant road, he walked along it.' "

Even if a person does not reach his goal, yet his heart ever seeks to attain it. I read the writings of Confucius, and I pictured to myself what sort of man he had been. I went to Lu, and in the temple of Chung Ni I contemplated his chariot, his garments, and his ceremonial implements. At a fixed time, scholars performed the rites of his house. So I remained there, full of reverence, and could not tear myself away. There were on earth many princes and sages who, in their lifetime, were famous, but whose names were no longer known after their death. Confucius was a simple man of the people. But after more than ten generations, his doctrine is still handed down, and men of learning honour him as Master. From the Son of Heaven, and from kings and princes on, all who practise the six free arts in the Middle Kingdom take their decisions and their measure from the Master. That can be designated the highest possible sanctity.

Chapter II

CRITICAL EXAMINATION OF THE DATA OF
SSE-MA CH'IEN. THE HISTORICAL SIGNIF-
ICANCE OF CONFUCIUS

THE biography of Confucius which Sse-Ma
Ch'ien noted down in the midst of the his-
tories of the individual states, as a special mark
of distinction, for the "uncrowned king," will
form the basis of the biographies of Confucius
for all time; for there was no chronologically
arranged biography of the Master before Sse-
Ma Ch'ien.

Nevertheless, Sse-Ma Ch'ien had his sources.
In the first place, the historical works from the
school of the Master himself came into consideration: the Commentaries of K'ung Yang and Ku
Liang on the Spring and Autumn Annals of Confucius. Sse-Ma Ch'ien also makes extensive use
of the History of Tso Ch'iu. This is divided, at
the present time, into the so-called Tso Chuan, in
which later scholars saw a commentary on the
Spring and Autumn Annals, and the Kuo Yü, that
is, Speeches from the Various States. Sse-Ma

Ch'ien makes use of both parts of this work, without taking offence at the miraculous character of some of the stories.[1]

Besides these works, he had at his disposal the notes from the Confucian camp, which we no longer possess in the form in which they came to him. One of these works, and one which he extensively used, is the Conversations of Confucius, known under the name of the Lun Yü.[2]

In its present form, this work is a product of the editorship of Chêng K'ang-chêng (127-200 A.D.) and therefore represents a later stratum than the work of Sse-Ma Ch'ien. But naturally, the recension of Chêng goes back to older sources, one of which is based upon oral tradition, while the other was published by the contemporary of Sse-Ma Ch'ien, the descendant of the Master, K'ung An-kuo, after a copy in old characters found in

[1] Cf. the story of the Fên sheep in the year 505 B.C., that of the great bone in the year 494, and that of the arrow with the stone head in the year 495.

[2] *Translators' Note.* Since Legge, the usual English title of this book is the *Analects of Confucius*, but Wilhelm's *Gespräche* (*Conversations*) is a much more accurate rendition.

the house of Confucius. Unfortunately, the question as to the value of this find has never been satisfactorily cleared up, since K'ung An-kuo fell into disfavour with the Emperor on account of a political law-suit in which he was involved, and, as Sse-Ma Ch'ien says, in his biography of Confucius, died before his time. His edition of the Lun Yü, as well as his other finds, was forgotten in the course of time; they were, in part, superseded by later forgeries. In Sse-Ma Ch'ien, we have many quotations from these Conversations, in a form which deviates in part from the edition known today, is often better than this, and, at any rate, casts considerable light on the text.

The utterances of the Lun Yü have, for the most part, to be sure, the form of short aphorisms, and it is often difficult to determine just how they should be historically arranged. Sse-Ma Ch'ien seems, in this matter, to have acted, for the most part, as he thought best. He combines his sources in mosaic fashion, even though he naturally had his reasons for the manner of his arrangement.

Besides the Lun Yü, he also had at hand the Chia Yü, or the School Conversations of Confucius, which were among the old writings edited by K'ung An-kuo.

We are worse off in respect to this work than in respect to the Lun Yü. Whereas our edition of the latter work offers, all in all, thoroughly reliable material, the Chia Yü exist in an edition from the third century A.D., which was published by Wang Sun, who died in the year 256 A.D. The great majority of the Chinese critics are of the opinion that the work was not edited by Wang Su, but actually written by him. However, he had sources, and, indeed, such sources as are still accessible to us at the present time. Almost every individual section of the Chia Yü can be run down in the literature of the centuries between Confucius and Wang Su. At the same time, however, the text of the Chia Yü has, for the most part, a form which cannot be traced back to the form of those texts that are now at our disposal. Chavannes, therefore, early came to the conclusion that the Chia Yü deserved more consideration than scholars, in the main, are willing to grant. At all events, it must never be forgotten that the matter which is handed down in the Chia Yü represents a second and often a third stratum of the tradition, and accordingly contains a large number of strongly mythical components.

Another source of similar character to the Chia Yü is the Book of Rites (Li Chi), which, in its present form, is a product of the Han times.

Sse-Ma Ch'ien naturally offers no criticism of his sources, but through the manner in which he uses them he indicates the degree of confidence with which he regards them. Those sources which seem to him more reliable he uses more frequently than the less reliable ones.

Thus he does not avoid occasionally using something from the literature of Taoism, and also even from the literature of the opponents of Confucius, when there is a strong tradition at hand. He mentions, for example, the visit of Confucius to Lao Tze in Chou, and from the Yen-Tze Ch'un Ch'iu he takes the warning with which Yen Ying, the Chancellor of Ch'i, is said to have estranged his prince from Confucius. This warning, which is also found in the writings of Mo Ti, surely does not arise from Yen Ying, who, as is reported in another place, once came to Lu, with his prince,

Ching, and there entered into friendly relations with Confucius.[1]

Other sources of doubtful reliability are also not avoided. Thus, the story of the musical studies of Confucius comes from Han Ying, a contemporary of Sse-Ma Ch'ien. This certainly does not belong in the place in which it is narrated. For the Music-Master, Hsiang, from whom Confucius learned to play the zither, is the same person whom he appointed Chief Musician when he was in power in Lu, and who, after the departure of Confucius from his native state, went into the ocean; that is, in all probability, retired to an island. The instruction in music must, then, have been earlier, and this corresponds to the entire body of facts regarding the situation.

A word must now be said regarding the chronological arrangement of events in Sse-Ma's biography of Confucius. There are obvious errors in the Shih Chi. Perhaps the most important error is the placing of the death of Mêng Hsi-chi in the year 535 B.C., instead of in 518, in which year his death is mentioned in the Ch'un Ch'iu. It can

[1] In the History of the State of Ch'i (Ch'i Shih Chia).

be observed that Sse-Ma Ch'ien's statement arises from a lack of care in the use of the Tso Chuan, since in that work there is a notice, under the date of 535, of the word which Mêng uttered at his death seventeen years later. Now it is obvious, without further discussion, that Confucius, at the age of seventeen, could not yet have attracted so much public attention that a dying official of high rank would have given him his son to educate. On the other hand, the whole problem is satisfactorily solved if we substitute the year 518. In that year Confucius was thirty-four years of age; that is, old enough to appear upon the scene as the teacher of pupils. There is a remarkable confirmation of this from another source. In the Li Chi, Confucius mentions an eclipse of the sun which occurred while he and Lao Tze were at a funeral.[1] Such an eclipse of the sun can actually be worked out for the year 518 B.C., so that everything harmonizes without doing any violence to the facts. Confucius was thirty-four years old when, with two young aristocrats, he travelled to the capital, and there, among other things, met Lao Tze. By

[1] Section Tsêng Tsi Wên.

means of this fixing of the date, we get a suitable period of time for the remaining events of his youth: his marriage, the birth of his son, the death of his mother, the expiration of the period of mourning, as well as for the petty offices which he held in the service of the Chi family, which last are the only possible explanation for the circumstance that Confucius was able to appear at a banquet that the Chi family gave to its officials. It is quite out of the question that Confucius, as a sixteen-year-old youth, should have shown the tactlessness to attempt to force himself, as if he were an adult, as guest at a banquet where he had no business to be, and this at a time when he was still wearing mourning. On the other hand, such a brutal snub of the young household official by a powerful vassal of the family would be quite readily understood when the latter was so rude as was Yang Hu.[1]

[1] The version which is found in the Chia Yü is also worthy of note: Confucius was in mourning for his mother. Yang Hu offered his condolences and said: "Have you heard that the Chi family is giving a feast today for all the honored men of the country?" Confucius replied: "No. I have heard nothing about it, or else I should have gone in spite of being in mourn-

The events which immediately followed: the fateful cock fight at the court of Lu, in 517 B.C., which terminated with the exile of Prince Chao of Lu, and the removal of Confucius to Ch'i, which is connected with this event, are historically unobjectionable, as is also the fact that Confucius left Ch'i again, after a period of useless waiting, to remain quietly in Lu, from 516 to 502 B.C., while the rebellions of Yang Hu (505 B.C.) and Kung-Shan Pu-niu (called in another place Kung-Shan Fu-yao) plunged the State of Lu into disorder. The following episode is also questionable: that Kung-Shan Pu-niu is said to have wished to summon Confucius during the rebellion, and that Confucius hesitated for a moment as to whether he should accept the call. Liang Ch'i Ch'ao, in his criticism of the Lun Yü, in which this epoch is also depicted, is of the opinion that there is a falsification at this point, since Confucius was actually the most dangerous opponent of Kung-

ing." Yang Hu is said to have rejoined: "No, that is not what I meant. The Chi family, which is inviting everybody, has left you out." In all probability, we here have the tale in an earlier stage of development, but even this is scarcely trustworthy.

79

Shan Pu-niu, whose fortress walls he indeed razed in 498 B.C. Be that as it may, there is certainly a question of disparity of time. Just as Yang Hu might possibly have wished to induce Confucius to enter his service, so also Kung-Shan Pu-niu might, perhaps, have attempted to do the same. From the very beginning, however, Confucius resolutely rejected all efforts toward a *rapprochement* on the part of Yang Hu, so that there is, in any case, a great probability that Confucius also took a clearly defined negative stand toward any similar proposals of Kung-Shan Pu-niu. For it must not be forgotten that it would have been a sort of treason on the part of Confucius if he had joined the rebels in his own state. The episode seems to be a doublet to the call through Pi Hsi, who was maintaining himself in Chung Mou against the attacks of Chao Chien-chi.[1] Here the situation was entirely different, since it was not a question of the native state of Confucius.[2]

[1] Lun Yü, XVII, 7.

[2] It may here be expressly mentioned that the execution of Shao Chêng-mao, after Confucius had come to power in Lu, is a forgery. This act is directly contrary to Confucius' entire

There now follows the period of the official activity of Confucius in Lu, which must have occurred between the years 501 and 496 B.C.

The period of the wanderings of Confucius which follows is naturally very difficult to arrange in chronological order. Here Sse-Ma Ch'ien seems to have juxtaposed his sources, rather than to have worked them over. This is indicated by the fact that various events are narrated twice; so, for example, the exclamation: "Let me go home!" This is given once in a version which follows the text of Mencius (VII, II, 37), and the second time for the year 492 B.C. (when Confucius was once more in Ch'ên), in a version which follows the Lun Yü (V, 21). It is, however, quite apparent that there can be no question of the possibility of two events, but that the same event is told twice. The same state of affairs exists in the case of the whole turn of events which precedes these words of Confucius.

After his departure from Lu, Confucius first went to Wei; from there to P'u, then again to

manner of conduct, and is probably first mentioned by Hsün Ch'ing.

Wei, where he lived in the house of Chü Po-yü; then, *via* Ts'ao, Sung, and Chêng, to Ch'ên, where he remained three years. It is then narrated that Ts'ai moved its capital into the district of Wu, and here follows, for the first time, the exclamation mentioned above.

The Master, however, has no thought of returning home, but betakes himself to P'u; from there—forced by an oath not to go to Wei, but ignoring this oath—to Wei. Then, after various vain attempts to find shelter elsewhere (with Po Hsi and in Chao—between which two events is found the story of the musical studies of Confucius, which are surely incorrectly placed), he again returns to Wei (sic!), at which time his sojourn with Chü Po-yü is once more mentioned. Then—leaving out the sojourns in Ts'ao, Sung, and Chêng—again to Ch'ên. The transfer of the capital of Ts'ai is mentioned once more. Then the words: "Let me go home!" follow for the second time. But this time, also, the Master does not go home, but goes to Ts'ai and from there to Shê! The difficulty arises between Ch'ên and Ts'ai, from which he is freed by Ch'u.

Even when we calculate the dates year by year the result is obvious that it must be a question of the same cycle of events. For his stay in Ts'ao, which coincides with the death of Duke Ting of Lu, we get the date 495 B.C.; then comes the journey through Sung and Chêng, and a three years' sojourn in Ch'ên, so that we arrive at the year 492. Now comes the journey via P'u and the new sojourn in Wei. Confucius "departs," wishes to go to Pi Hsi in Chung Mou, but does not carry out his intention; he plays the musical stones, learns to play the lute, is about to go to Chao and turns back again (all this while still in Wei). He discusses government with Duke Ling of Wei, then journeys to Ch'ên, and, in the year 493, when Ling of Wei dies, and in 492, when the temples of Dukes Huan and Hsi of Lu are burned down, he is still to be found there.

It is clear that the entire chronology is hopelessly confused, and that the only solution to the riddle is to postulate two sources which are joined together, one after another, and which narrate the same events, with slight deviations. We actually have a similar case at the very beginning of the

83

biography, where the whole life is anticipatorily depicted in large outlines, before the journey to the capital of Chou is narrated.

Even though one attempts, by means of redisposition, to arrange the order of events on the basis of one definite source, no sure result that is free from all objections will ever be attained.[1]

A life of Confucius such as can be presented on the basis of the sources can give with certainty only the larger features: after a sojourn in his youth in Lu, which is interrupted by a journey to the imperial capital, and by a stay in Ch'i (which was not broken up, in all probability, through the friendly minister, Yen Ying, but by other intrigues), there follows a short but brilliant period of official activity on the part of the Master in his native state. He attains important successes in foreign affairs (as the meeting of the princes in Chia Ku); and he is also successful in enforcing the authority of the central power upon the rebellious aristocracy by a clever use of their

[1] In the book on Confucius published by Frohmann, I attempted to give the chronology according to the statements of the Chinese work, K'ung Tze Pien Nien, which is based upon the Ch'un Ch'iu.

domestic difficulties, though it must be emphasized that the success was not so complete as tradition later on portrayed it to be. Likewise, he succeeds in restoring order and morality throughout public life, so that the State of Lu, which had fallen into complete anarchy, took an upward curve that aroused the envy of its neighbours.

It is important to bear in mind these practical successes of Confucius in order not to see in him merely the learned pedant, but to recognize that he possessed in the highest degree, and on the basis of serious labour, the technique for regulating humanity; and that only the adverse conditions of the times and not a lack of ability on the part of Confucius prevented him from being ranked as one of the active social reformers of China. It is from the point of view of these successes and of the thoroughly justified self-consciousness and professional spirit on the part of Confucius that his long, vain attempts to find an opportunity, while in the service of a prince, to make use of his talents are explicable. The time when he made these attempts—the period of his wanderings—is concentrated around the State of

Wei and the territories lying to the south of it. Prince Ling of Wei was, in all probability, sensual, and—as is usually the case with those given over to sensuality—weak. But he had understanding for the teachings of Confucius, and, as it seems, a certain personal affection for him as well. Nevertheless, this period of his life, so full of want and disappointment, was, in the last analysis, only an interlude. But even if this period was externally a failure, it bore rich inner fruits for Confucius. One must call to mind the passage in Mencius:

"Thus, when Heaven is about to confer a great office on any man, it first exercises his mind with suffering, and his sinews and bones with toil. It exposes his body to hunger, and subjects him to extreme poverty. It confounds his undertakings. By all these methods it stimulates his mind, hardens his nature, and supplies his incompetencies. . . . From these things we see how life springs from sorrow and calamity, and death from ease and pleasure." [1]

[1] Mencius, Book VI, Part II, Chapter XV, ¶ 2, 5.

Translators' Note. The English of this paragraph from Mencius is that of Legge's translation, Chinese Classics, Vol. II, p. 447.

In Chuang Tze, there occurs a remarkable indication of a great change which took place in the
Master in his sixtieth year.[1] This change might
very well be connected with the expression which
has already been quoted so frequently: "Let me go
home!" At all events, there are various indica-
tions that he finally decided to relinquish his long
and vain attempts to create order by the use of

[1] Chuang Tze, XXVII, 2.

Translators' Note. The English from Wilhelm's translation
of this section of Chuang Tze follows:

The Change in Confucius. Chuang Tze said to Hui Tze:
"Confucius had lived to be sixty years old, but in his sixtieth
year a change came over him. That which he at first considered
right, in the end he considered false. We do not know whether
we shall also, after our fifty-ninth year, consider false that
which we today consider right."

Hui Tze said: "Confucius surrendered himself to learning
with ardent determination."

Chuang Tze said: "Confucius had long before left that path.
That which Confucius was wont to say: 'Man has received his
talents from the great First Cause. His soul must be born again
for life. The song must be in accord with the pitch; the words
must be in accord with the law. When gain and duty are spread
out before a man, one can judge of his predilections and aver-
sions,' those are all words which find the external recognition
of mankind, nothing more. But that he has found the inner
recognition of mankind, so that no one dared to set himself
up against him, for having given the world its fixed regulations
—enough, enough! I shall never equal him."—Page 208.

87

the rites and rules of antiquity. It is quite possible that the Taoistic hermits, a considerable number of whom he had met, and who were always preaching withdrawal from the world, exerted a certain influence upon him. Out of the conscientious, optimistic mediator of antiquity and the tirelessly active reformer, there grew, at all events, after his return to the quiet of private life in his native state of Lu, a calm philosopher of great superiority, who devoted himself to the study of the esoteric teachings of the Book of Changes, and who created for the world, in his Spring and Autumn Annals, his program for government— what might be called the foundation plan of Chinese culture; while, at the same time, he handed down to living tradition, through personal instruction to his students, whatever he left behind in the way of written memorials, which were to carry his heritage down to the future through the storms of the succeeding centuries.

If, at the conclusion of this section, we raise a question as to the personality of Confucius, it must be confessed that the answer is not easy, for any one of the present generation. For it is our high regard for active and effectual power which, most of all, separates us from those times and from that cultural period. For us, originality, progress, innovation, change, the revolutionary and the individualistic count as great. And in Confucius there is, at first sight, absolutely nothing to attract our attention. Indeed, he seems only to endeavour to avoid every suspicion of desiring anything new, of desiring anything else but to love the old, to hand down, and to "make" nothing. A great number of statements by him are available which point in this direction. In the same way, we see him busied with the ancient writings. His interest is directed particularly to them. He practises the manners of antiquity, and he seeks, through a more and more comprehensive learning and practice, to put himself in possession of the forces of the past, convinced that those forces are eternal forces which also rule the future. And so it is no wonder that, in his eyes, the highest of all virtues is respect, piety [1] in the presence of the old and the past, the continuation and completion of which is

[1] *Translators' Note.* Piety in the Vergilian sense (*pius Aeneas*).

the duty of succeeding generations. Thus he did not become a scholar, but a learner; he did not become a polyhistor, but a philosopher. And through the practice and learning of manners and of tradition, there grows increasingly in the later years of his life a sovereign control of the laws of life, of which he was aware by virtue of the revelation from within, and in connection with the old and mysterious Book of Changes. And so we find in Confucius, in his very old age, an ascending development in the direction in which Lao Tze before him had found his Way.

This growth of a personality, starting on a plane which is accessible to every one, into metaphysical depths, is something that lies outside the immediate realm of Occidental judgment, because we have accustomed ourselves to rate especially high immediate talent that requires no learning to reach its goal. But in this case we must not use our present standards of measurement if we wish to be just; we must rather, on the one hand, take into consideration the work, and, on the other hand, the effect, in order to be able to pass judgment as to whether Confucius was or was not a great man.

There can be no difference of opinion concerning the influence of Confucius in China, indeed in the entire Far East. Even during his lifetime he made an indelible impression upon both his immediate and his more distant disciples. They loved and honored him like a father and even the princes and grandees of his time never had any doubt as to his personal greatness, and only human, all too human, reasons kept them from his train. The manner in which Confucius has made himself felt in the course of the centuries, and in spite of all obstacles, shows still further the greatness of his influence. It can be confidently said that the greatness of his influence is in direct ratio to an understanding of his personality. Nothing, perhaps, attests more strongly to this influence than the inner change which James Legge, the Christian missionary, experienced. Legge entered upon his work with the Confucian classics, labouring under every possible prejudice; but he possessed the courage of an inborn desire for truth. In the first edition of his work, in 1861, he epitomizes his judgment thus: "It is impossible for me to regard him as a great man." [1] But thirty-two years later, in 1893, he writes: ". . . the more I have studied his character and opinions, the more highly have I come to regard him. He was a very great man, and his influence has been on the whole a great benefit to the Chinese, while his teachings suggest important lessons to ourselves who profess to belong to the school of Christ." [2]

History gives us information concerning the work of Confucius. Confucius stands at a turning-point in Chinese history. The old feudal culture that had as its point of departure a succession of "saints on the throne" had broken down. Confucius takes up the thread, although he was a man of the people. Thus he marks that point in Chinese history where the guidance of society passed from the theocratic ruler to the human philosopher. Confucius founded the first private school, which gave not only occasional instruction of a master to such students as happened to live in his house, but also offered a systematic education for

[1] *Translators' Note.* The English is a translation of Wilhelm's translation, since the 1861 edition of Legge was not available.

[2] *Translators' Note.* James Legge, *The Chinese Classics*, Vol. I, p. 111.

public activity in the ruling of state and society.
What this example, which was afterwards imitated
by many philosophers, meant, what power could
be exercised through such a school, can be most
clearly seen from the fact that Ch'in Shih Huang
Ti initiated his fight against Confucius just at this
point.[1] The Emperor demanded that the old documents which these schools of learning were using
as texts should be destroyed, and that the private
training of officials should give way to a public
system, conducted and inspected by the State; for
he recognized the power which lay in the educa-
tional system of Confucius. In spite of his vehe-
ment attempts, the First Emperor did not succeed
in accomplishing his will. His dynasty was scattered
to the four winds, but the Confucian system of
education for leaders persisted for thousands of
years. And while China, through the entire course
of its history, was in form an absolute monarchy,
it was in reality a republic which was ruled by an
aristocracy of the spirit, and which had behind it

[1] *Translators' Note.* Ch'in Shih Huang Ti, the first emperor
of the Ch'in Dynasty, usually called "The First Emperor"; the
"builder" of the Great Wall.

93

the enormous power of the tradition founded by Confucius. To be sure, the authority of this aristocracy was not unlimited. Often enough, times arose when the final decision lay with the sword. But after such crises there always followed periods of peace, during which the guardians of the spirit could exercise their influence.

Naturally this republic of scholars and their power became great in the course of a gradual development, and it is likewise clear that the trend was not always unified, but that there were frequent schisms, though all this does not change the broad general outline. And when considering such phenomena, one is sure to go astray if one attempts to regard them as something which, in the last analysis, is a product of chance. Confucianism without Confucius is quite as unhistorical as Christianity without Christ. At the very root of a life so entirely personally constituted, there must lie certain mighty forces in order to enable that life constantly to develop and endure. If a certain stage of civilization is founded by "Gods," there are other stages, in the centre of which heroes, prophets, saints—in short, human beings—are to be found. And these forms are inconceivable without a powerful human representative. For this reason, the work of Confucius is a proof of his greatness. And the circumstance that this work was expanded and developed by later generations does not detract from this greatness.

Chapter III

THE DOCUMENTS CONTAINING THE CONFUCIAN TEACHINGS

THE CLASSICS

CONFUCIUS himself wrote nothing; even in the field of literature, his activity was that of handing down the traditional, rather than creating something new. This was not due to lack of originality or creative power, but was connected with very special Chinese traditions. The great regulations for human conduct originated with the authorities appointed for that purpose; in the final analysis, from the Son of Heaven. For these regulations were no empty words or mere proposals of reform, but they were deeds, life-moulds, which were effectual through their innate legality; and people regulated their conduct in accordance with them because they were intrinsically authoritative. Confucius also had before him the goal of creating such moulds of life. He had no literary ends in view; he sought deeds, effects, creations. Here, then, he was in an extremely difficult situation. In the book on Measure and Mean,[1] we read: "If a man occupies the throne, but does not possess the necessary power of the spirit, he ought not to venture to undertake changes in civilization. Nor can one, even though he has the necessary power of the spirit, but not the highest authority, venture to undertake changes in civilization."[2]

Confucius was conscious of possessing the power of the spirit, which gave him a right to a re-creation of civilization. But such absolutely necessary external authority as would have permitted him to exercise that power was the thing which was lacking: he was, after all, only "the man from Chou," a simple bourgeois in a cloth gown, nowhere an external sanction to deliver the message that he wished to bring; that he was, indeed, im-

[1] Chung Yung, Chap. XXVIII.

Translators' Note. Usually known in English as *The Doctrine of the Mean.*

[2] *Translators' Note.* Legge's translation deviates appreciably from Wilhelm's. The latter translates *tê* as *Kraft des Geistes,* whereas Legge retains the more conventional meaning, *virtue.* Legge is also more literal, and has for *li yüeh, ceremonies and music,* which Wilhelm renders by *Kultur.* Legge's note to the passage, however, indicates that he understands the two ideograms in a somewhat broader sense, though not quite as Wilhelm interprets them.

97

pelled to bring. It was for that reason that he made so long and vain a search to find a prince who might have given him the necessary authority to carry out all the reforms in the life of humanity which had become necessary since the last culture-creation—that of the Chou Dynasty—had collapsed. But, as has already been mentioned, no such prince could be found. Now Confucius might have written literary works in which to precipitate his thoughts. He would then have had a place in the long line of poets and scholars who have sought to react upon posterity through the setting up of a Utopia. He did not travel this road; he desired to be of influence, not merely to write.

This is the probable reason why, as K'ang Yu-wei has quite convincingly shown, he supported his ideas of reform by giving them out, not as his own ideas, but by surrounding them with the authority of the greatest antiquity and of its wisest rulers. This was the reason why he "only transmitted and did not create." For in the garb of the authority of the greatest antiquity, these teachings were bound to claim an importance which they did not deserve from the standpoint of their inner content.[1] We see quite clearly that Confucius here entered upon a new path. It is said that Lao Tze mocked him on this account and advised him to cast out of his hands the mould which was all that remained of the ancient times. But Confucius was not to be deterred. He faithfully collected and sifted: from the times of the rulers Yao and Shun, whose dates are usually placed near 2300 B.C., down to the establishment of the Chou Dynasty, he subjected everything to an intensive study. And finally he so edited the remnants of antiquity that they became the principal witnesses of his doctrine.

a. *The Book of Records* [2]

The first book which Confucius edited in this fashion was the Book of Records, called in Chinese the Shang Shu or Shu Ching. There is, at the present time, a great controversy among sinologists regarding this work and its genuineness, and

---

[1] In this appeal to antiquity for the purpose of the authorization of his own teachings, Confucius has had imitators. Mo Ti made the great Yü his authority; others, for example, the agrarian communists, made the Divine Husbandman [Shên Nung] theirs.

[2] Usually called the Book of History. [*Tr.*]

this controversy seems to tend more and more against the authenticity of the work as a whole. The state of the case is somewhat as follows: The Book of Records, as we possess it today, contains decrees, which, beginning with the ruler Yao, whose date is usually put in the twenty-fourth century B.C., carry us down into the Chou Dynasty, to the address of Duke Mu of Ch'in to his ministers, in the year 629 B.C.[1]

We have no knowledge of the sources which Confucius had at his disposal for his edition of the book. It appears that the historiography of antiquity was divided between two officials, one a Historian of the Left, and one a Historian of the Right. Of these two, the one had the duty of recording the acts; the other, that of recording the speeches. The one activity would accordingly correspond to that of a chronicler; the other, to that of a secretary. The records do not have the form of chronicles, but are rather documents dealing with all sorts of events and negotiations within

[1] *Translators' Note.* Chinese authorities today do not regard Yao and Shun (*supra*) as historical personages. See p. 172, and Franke, Vol. I, p. 71.

100

the government then in control. These documents, however, are not preserved in their original form. At least, the introductory words speak of an "investigation of antiquity." The fact that the great seal character, which was used at the time of Confucius, was not invented until the year 800 B.C. must also be taken into consideration. That a form of writing existed in China earlier than that time has recently been proved beyond a doubt by finds of incised bones which were used for purposes of divination, and which are at least as old as the twelfth century before Christ. But it may easily be supposed that the text suffered severely from its transcription into the new style ideograms. We see from what point of view Confucius edited the text when we compare other transmissions which concern the same period.[1] Whereas in those other accounts there are tales of wild wars and murders, even in the earliest periods, with victory or defeat often extremely uncertain, the documents of the Book of Records contain wise regulations of sainted rulers, or lofty admonitions of faithful ministers, after hearing which, the ruler meditates and does

[1] Cf. especially, the Bamboo Annals.

penance. Nevertheless, even in the Book of Records, a sufficient amount of bloody wars is in evidence in the account of the most sainted of the rulers to cause a Mencius of a later day to doubt, on moral grounds, the veracity of this book.

But the worst feature of the situation is that we absolutely no longer possess that Book of Records which Confucius used for the instruction of his pupils. About the middle of the third century before Christ, the tyrant, Ch'in Shih Huang Ti, caused all the historical records of antiquity to be burned. Only in the Imperial Library was one copy of each work of that category to be preserved. The Book of Records was among the books burned at that time. By this burning of the books, the Emperor wished to silence the criticism in the form of an appeal to antiquity which was being levelled at him by scholars. But even the individual copies in the Imperial Library were not preserved, because, in the bloody struggles that followed the Ch'in Dynasty, the Imperial palace, with all its treasures, was sacrificed to the flames.

Meantime, a new form of writing was again introduced, which, with minor variations, is current even at the present day. When the times gradually grew more peaceful under the succeeding Han Dynasty, men's thoughts turned back to the works of antiquity. Only fragments of the Book of Records came to light, and these fragments, it was said, rested on the oral tradition of the old scholar, Fu Shêng, who had learned the texts by heart in his youth. These texts were then written down in the new ideograms which were current at that time.

Later on it was alleged that new finds had been made in the walls of the old house of Confucius, but these were all written in the old characters, which, meanwhile, had long been forgotten. As has already been mentioned, a descendant of Confucius, K'ung An-kuo, published these texts, after transferring them into the modern ideogram and providing them with commentaries. The find was not universally accepted as genuine. A controversy arose between the schools of the so-called new text (that is, those texts which were found earlier and were written in the "new" character), and of the so-called old text (that is, those texts which were found later and were written in the "old" character). K'ung An-kuo, the chief defender of the old text, was, however, involved in a political intrigue which ruined him; and his find seems also to have disappeared once more. Not until later did fragments come to light which were written in the old character, and which, it was claimed, went back to the find of K'ung An-kuo, but which were regarded by many scholars as forgeries. As time went on, the material became more and more abundant. So late as the Chin Dynasty, far into the Christian era, new finds were made, the genuineness of which, however, became more and more doubtful. As a general rule, it is now supposed that the so-called new text contains the relatively more reliable parts of the book— that is, those which lead back to the proximity of Confucius himself!—and that, on the other hand, the sections which are found only in the so-called old text are untrustworthy. The sections of the new text are the following chapters: 1. The Canon of Yao, 2. The Counsel of Kao Yao, 3. The Tribute of Yü, 4. The Speech in Kan, 5. The Speech of T'ang, 6. Pan Kung, 7. The Day of Sacrifice of Kao Tsung, 8. The Conquest of Li by

the Margrave of the West, 9. The Count of Wei,
10. The Great Pronouncement, 11. The Pronouncement of Mu, 12. The Great Rule, 13. The
Metal Bound Chest, 14. The Great Announcement, 15. The Announcement to K'ang, 16. The
Announcement Concerning Drunkenness, 17. The
Beam of Tsi Wood, 18. The Announcement of
Shao, 19. The Announcement Concerning Lo, 20.
The Numerous Officials, 21. Against Luxury,
22. Prince Shih, 23. The Various Regions, 24. On
the Organization of the Government, 25. The Last
Will, 26. Liu on Punishments, 27. The Message
to Prince Wên, 28. The Address at Pei, 29. The
Address of the Duke of Ch'in. In addition to the
above, there are twenty-nine further sections of
the so-called old text, so that we have, in all,
fifty-eight sections, whereas the text of Confucius is said to have contained one hundred sections.

The spirit of the entire work is strictly ethical.
We find the principles of Confucius repeated
throughout. Nevertheless, there is still a glimmer-
ing of very primitive conditions. Thus, there seems
to have prevailed a sort of astronomic religion,

with a Priest-King at its head.[1] In the earliest times, the new ruler was not the son of his predecessor, but was chosen by the ruler in consultation with the grandees of the court, and was then led, as regent, in solemn ceremony, before his lofty ancestor and god.

With the exception of those oldest portions, the most important part of the Book of Records is the so-called Hung Fan, the Great Plan, in which is given a mythico-metaphysical cosmology, in connection with a system for the regulation of human society. The following is a translation of the section:

"Heaven gave Yü the great rule, with its nine divisions, whereby the interrelation of duties was made clear: 1. The Five States of Change, 2. The Careful Execution of the Five Actions, 3. The Serious Application of the Eight Means of Government, 4. The Harmonious Application of the Five Arrangements, 5. The Edifying Application of the Sublime Pole, 6. The Cultivated Applica-

[1] *Translators' Note.* Cf. Bruno Schindler, *Das Priestertum im alten China.* 1. Teil, *Königtum und Priestertum. Einleitung und Quellen.* Leipzig, 1919.

tion of the Three Virtues, 7. The Intelligent Application of the Examination of Doubts, 8. The Thoughtful Application of the Various Signs, 9. The Stimulating Application of the Five Types of Happiness, and the Awe-inspiring Application of the Six Sufferings.

"1. The Five States of Changes are: (1) The State of Water, (2) The State of Fire, (3) The State of Wood, (4) The State of Metal, (5) The State of the Earth. Water seeps downward, fire flickers upward, wood can bend and stretch, metal follows a mould, the earth creates the seedtime and the harvest. By means of that which seeps downward, a salty taste is engendered; by means of that which flickers upward, a bitter taste is engendered; through the bending and stretching, a sour taste is engendered; through that which follows a mould, a sharp taste is engendered; through seedtime and harvest, a sweet taste is engendered.

"2. The Five Actions are: Mien, Speech, Seeing, Hearing, Thinking. Let the mien be serious, the speech suitable, the gaze clear; let hearing be penetrating and thinking sharp. Seriousness brings about dignity, suitability brings about order, clarity brings about wisdom, penetration brings about counsel, sharpness brings about sanctity.

"3. The Eight Means of Government are: Food, Goods, Sacrifices, Labour, Instruction, Protection Against Crime, Entertainment of Guests, and the Army.

"4. The Five Arrangements are: the Year, the Moon, the Day, the Stars and their Houses, the Calendric Calculations.

"5. The Sublime Pole is: the Exercise of Government Through the Person of the Sovereign (abridged).

"6. The Three Virtues are: The first, Simplicity and Justice; the second, Strict Rule, the third, Mild Rule. During peace and prosperity, let simplicity and justice rule; against force and rebellion strict rule serves; in the face of harmony and friendliness, mild rule serves. Against those who are shrewd and secretive, strict rule serves; toward those who are highminded and distinguished, mild rule serves.—Let the ruler alone create happiness; let the ruler alone have costly viands. The officials should not be able to create happiness, nor to create fear, nor to have costly viands. If the officials create happiness and fear, or have costly viands, it will injure your house, and it bodes ill for your kingdom. For then the vassals are partisan and prejudiced, and the common people become impertinent and presumptuous.

"7. The Announcement of Doubts is: Let augurs be selected and appointed for the tortoise and the millefoil, and let them be commanded to consult the oracle of the tortoise and the millefoil. The tortoise shows the signs of rain, of clearing up, of cloudy weather, of separation, and of crossing. The millefoil oracle shows the signs for constancy and remorse. In all, there are seven signs, five of which are used in connection with the tortoise, two in connection with the millefoil, in order that the thirty errors may be adjusted. During the period when the tortoise and the millefoil are being interrogated, three men interpret the augury, and let the words of two of them be followed. If you are in great doubt, take counsel with your own heart, take counsel with your councillors and knights, take counsel with the common people,

take counsel with the oracle of the tortoise and the
millefoil. If you are for it, if the tortoise is for it,
if the millefoil is for it, if the councillors and
knights are for it, and if the common people are
for it: that is the great communality; this will
bring to your person health and strength, and will
create good fortune for your children and grand-
children. If you are for it, if the tortoise is for it,
if the millefoil is for it, but the councillors and the
knights are against it, and if the common people
are against it, the result will be fortunate. If councillors and knights are for it, if the tortoise is for
it, if the millefoil is for it, but you are against it,
and the common people are against it, the result
will be fortunate; if the common people are for
it, if the tortoise is for it, if the millefoil is for it,
but you are against it, and the councillors and
knights are against it, the result will be fortunate.
If you are for it, if the tortoise is for it, but the
millefoil is against it, if the councillors and knights
are against it, and if the common people are against
it, a fortunate outcome is indicated in internal affairs, an unfortunate outcome in external affairs.
If tortoise and millefoil agree but are opposed

to the people's opinion, a fortunate outcome is indicated for inaction, but an unfortunate outcome for action.

"8. The Various Signs are: Rain, Sunshine, Heat, Cold, Wind, and Seasonableness. If all five obtain, and each is in its proper order, then all plants will grow luxuriantly. If, however, one of these is excessively strong, it is an indication of evil; and if one is absolutely lacking, it is also an indication of evil. There are favourable signs: Seriousness, which is shown when the rain comes seasonably; Order, which is shown when sunshine comes in due season; Wisdom, which is shown when heat comes in due season; Good Counsel, which is shown when cold comes in due season; Holiness, which is shown when the wind comes in due season. But there are also evil signs: Recklessness, which is shown when there is constant rain; Haughtiness, which is shown when there is constant sunshine; Frivolity, which is shown when there is constant heat; Hastiness, which is shown when there is constant cold; Stupidity, which is shown when there is constant wind.

"The king observes the year, the councillors and knights observe the month, the retinue of underlings observe the day. If there is no change of seasonableness in year, month, and day, all the fruits of the field will become mature, deeds are clear, bold heroes distinguish themselves, and peace and prosperity reign in all families. If the seasonableness constantly changes in year, month, and day, all the fruits of the field will not mature, foolish and unwise deeds will be performed, heroes will conceal themselves, and the families will become restless.

"The common people are like the stars. Among the stars, there are such as love the wind and such as love the rain. The courses of the sun and moon bring about winter and summer. If the moon follows the stars, wind and rain are the result.

"9. The Five Types of Happiness: The first Happiness is Long Life, the second is Affluence, the third is Health and Repose, the fourth is Love of Virtue, the fifth is the Completion of One's Years of Life. The Six Sufferings are: the first is Misfortune which cuts off life, the second is Sickness, the third is Care, the fourth is Poverty, the fifth is Wickedness, the sixth is Weakness."[1]

b. *The Book of Odes*[2]

The Book of Odes belongs to the most reliable and best-preserved works of Chinese literature. Modern sinology, which, as before mentioned, regards the Book of Records with complete scepticism, universally recognizes the Book of Odes as a historical source. In the following paragraphs there is a presentation of the latest investigations by Liang Ch'i Ch'ao on the Book of Odes.

Tradition has it that, at the time of Confucius, there were supposed to be 3,000 old songs extant, from which he selected 300 as of value for virtue and morals, while rejecting the rest. But if we take into consideration the statement of Confucius

[1] *Translators' Note.* Legge's translation of The Great Plan is found in Vol. III of *The Sacred Books of the East,* edited by F. Max Müller, pp. 137-149. Wilhelm's translation differs in several details and in the general point of view.

[2] *Translators' Note.* The Shih Ching is translated by Wilhelm as *Lieder* (*Songs*), but the book is generally known in English under the above caption, as in Legge. As will be seen from the text, the word *ode,* as a term for a formal song, applies only to certain of the poems.

himself, we obtain a different picture. He speaks quite naturally of the 300 songs as of an already existing collection. What he attributes to himself is merely the arrangement and the proper placing of the melodies to the songs already existent, and in Sse-Ma Ch'ien also (though he, by the way, mentions the sifting of the 3,000 songs) there is a statement that Confucius brought the music of the Book of Odes into harmony with the ancient music.

The Book of Odes contains 305 compositions, for several of which, to be sure, there are only titles without text. It is supposed that, in the case of these latter, it was a question of music for an orchestra, but without words. Unfortunately, the melodies of Confucius for the songs of the Book of Odes have been lost in the course of time, as, indeed, the ancient music which Confucius regarded most highly as a means of moral education, has, in the course of time, fallen into disuse.[1]

But besides this activity in the field of music, Confucius made the lyrics his own in still another

[1] *Translators' Note.* Mr. D. K. Lieu, an authority on Chinese music, is of the opinion that modern Chinese music, which was introduced from Greece via India, has no connection whatever with the ancient Chinese musical forms.

way, for he discussed and explained them in his daily intercourse with his students. In this way, he created a thoroughly firm tradition for the interpretation of the songs, and thereby a collection of songs was turned into a classical document, which was interpreted as if it contained the teachings of Confucius. This tradition was also very important from an historical point of view, in so far as this valuable portion of ancient Chinese literature would long since have been lost had it not been cherished, explained, and handed down by the School of Confucius. For, besides the Book of Odes, all the poetry that has come to us from Chinese antiquity is only a pitiful remnant, not even the date of which can be accurately determined.

Naturally, the manner of and the purpose in transmitting these songs to posterity contributed to the fact that the traditional explanation of the Odes had less consideration for their original meaning than for an allegorical interpretation which was attributed to them in order that they might fit into the system. Just as the Jewish records were transmitted in the Christian church, but were adapted to the new doctrine by an allegorical interpretation of their meaning, so the songs of the olden days were treated in the School of Confucius. It happened quite early that individual poets represented the relationship in which they stood to their prince by the picture of a deserted wife. Through this figure, allegorical songs arose which, under the guise of a love affair, portrayed political and social relations of another sort. The more the songs of antiquity served the School of Confucius as pedagogical material, the more the allegorical interpretation was emphasized; and, in the course of centuries, something quite different was made of the text from what it originally signified.

In its present form, the Book of Odes is divided into four parts: I. Folk Songs, which are composed of the two parts, the Chou Nan and the Shao Nan, and of the thirteen sections of the Kuo Fêng; 2. The Minor Songs of Ya; 3. The Major Songs of Ya; 4. The Sung, or Songs of Praise.[1]

[1] *Translators' Note.* 2, 3, and 4, above, are translated by Legge as: Minor Odes of the Kingdom, Greater Odes of the Kingdom, Odes of the Temple and the Altar. For the sake of

Liang Ch'i-Ch'ao, however, seems to have proved that this division is not the original one. Most probably, the Nan Songs formed the first part. There is every probability that the word *nan*, the usual meaning of which is *south*, is here used in an applied sense, and would then signify a solo, with a succeeding tutti of the accompanying instruments. It would here be necessary to investigate in how far the refrainlike repetitions at the beginning or end of the stanzas of many of these songs had any connection with the music and point to an alternation of solo and chorus. The Kuo Fêng (Manners of the Various States) formed the second part. They are rhymed stanzas which were not sung, but were recited in a rhythmical speaking voice, as is still the case in China with certain poems. These folk poems, which had their origin in various feudal states, were, if tradition may be trusted, gathered by the central government, in order to learn the manners and the mood of the

complete accuracy, it should be mentioned that the title, Kuo Fêng, which means *the manners of* or *the lessons from the states*, is applied to the entire first part, and that the two sets of Nan Songs and the thirteen Miscellaneous Odes of the States are both subtitles.

various parts of the country. These parts contain delightfully naïve folk-songs, which lead us to conclude that there were, at that time, decidedly freer manners in China than was usual later on. Because of these freer manners, the allegorical interpretation of the Book of Odes, which comes from the Confucian School of a later time, and which refers every love poem to a faithful official, or to the fame of a princess, or to the castigation of immorality, seems all the more strange. Modern sinology has rightly cast aside the prejudices which, for so long a time, stood in the way of a real understanding of these folk-songs. The Ya or Art Songs form the third part of the Book of Odes.[1] These were, in all probability, songs with instrumental accompaniment. The five songs which have titles but no texts were probably solo pieces for the orchestra. It is not strange that there are many points of contact between the Ya songs and

[1] *Translators' Note.* Legge admits that *Minor Odes of the Kingdom* is not a translation of *Ya*, and says that the word is explained by *Chêng, correct.* According to Legge, also, the Ya were produced in the royal territory.

the folk-songs. Even in later times, the art poetry of China has again and again drawn from the inexhaustible spring of the folk-songs. The Sung formed the fourth part of the Book of Odes. These were religious hymns, in part from antiquity, which were sung at the royal sacrificial feasts.

Upon what a lofty plane religion was in those ancient days is shown, for example, by such a song as the following, taken from the Sacrificial Odes of Chou, which reproduces the sacrificial carmen of the young king:

"Honour him, honour him!
　The revealed God!
　His will is hard!
　Say not: He is so high and far!
　He rises up and floats down,
　And daily sees our deeds.
　I am still young,
　An inexperienced fool.
　But day by day
　I strive aloft toward wisdom's light.

Help me to bear the burden!
Show me life's revelation!" [1]

c. *The Data on Manners*

Just as records and songs had an assured position in the School of Confucius, so manners also played a great rôle. We are, unfortunately, not in the happy position of being able here to point in the same way to a work upon which Confucius based his instruction. There are, to be sure, two works extant which occupy themselves with the manners of the Chou Dynasty: the so-called Chou

---

[1] *Translators' Note.* Legge's translation, Vol. IV, Part II, pp. 598-599, is as follows:

Let me be reverent, let me be reverent (in attending to my
  duties);
(The way of) Heaven is evident,
And its appointment is not easily (preserved).
Let me not say that it is high aloft above me.
It ascends and descends about our doings;
It daily inspects us wherever we are.

I am (but as) a little child,
Without intelligence to be reverently (attentive to my duties);
I will learn to hold fast the gleams (of knowledge), till I
  arrive at bright intelligence.
Assist me to bear the burden (of my position),
And show me how to display a virtuous conduct.

Li or Chou Kuan, and the I Li. Indeed, there was a time when these works were all, directly or indirectly, ascribed to the authorship of Confucius. But science today is of an entirely different opinion. The Chou Li turns out to be the account of an official system of the bureaucratic regulations of the Chou Dynasty, while the I Li contains rather the individual rules for correct conduct on special occasions. The great question is whether we are really dealing with works which actually do go back as far as the time of Confucius, and in this matter modern Sinology is more and more inclined to designate them as later forgeries. In Confucius' day there was, without doubt, a traditional set of manners and rules that had been officially introduced. But it is much less certain whether there were any written data on the subject or whether everything here rested upon oral tradition. The trouble which Confucius took, wherever opportunity offered, to make inquiry with regard to the rules of correct behaviour, rather leads to the conclusion that written data, even if they were available, were extremely meagre in character. In the School of Confucius notes were then made on manners. These notes, which were very mixed in content, were then later collected and published. In the Han period, there were two such collections by two scholars, the older and the younger Tai. The extant Li Chi (Notes on Manners) goes back to these collections, and contains material from very different times; in large majority, however, from the post-Confucian period. Nevertheless, we have in this work, also, which is usually reckoned as one of the Confucian Classics, a precipitate of that which Confucius thought and taught on the subject of manners. Next to manners, music also plays an important rôle for Confucius. For, if manners supplied the fixed forms under which life could be carried on, then music was destined to harmonize the feelings, and, at the same time, to arouse them in the desired direction. It has been seen in the biography of Confucius how intensively he lived in the world of music, so that he even forgot eating and drinking because of it. But we today can no longer pass judgment upon just this phase of Confucius' activity. It has disappeared without a trace. For music is the most transitory element of every civilization. Born of the most delicate emotions of the soul, it can be propagated only by immediate transfer from one person to another. Particularly in ancient China, where the musicians were for the most part blind men who reproduced the tones that they heard without the aid of notes, the interruption of the tradition, even for the space of one generation, was sufficient to destroy the entire catenation. And such interruptions occurred in sufficiently large number, during the restless centuries which witnessed the dissolution of the ancient order of society, to cause the demolition of ancient music. This is especially true since, even in Confucius' lifetime, other melodies, which he could only regard with the gravest suspicion, began to force their way to public attention.

Here we come to a point where we must renounce. The very finest and most beautiful part of the work of Confucius is destroyed. Mere jotted fragments of thoughts and rules are all that is left. But these notes still possess a strong dynamic inspiration for all who, without bias, yield to their influence.

d. *The Book of Changes*

In the last years of his life, Confucius occupied himself chiefly with the Book of Changes (I Ching). This book, which escaped the conflagration of Ch'in Shih Huang Ti, because it was a book of divination, exhibits, even so, in its present condition, a very uneven state of the text. The actual text is comparatively well preserved. It consists of sixty-four signs, which were originally intended for the oracle with the millefoil.[1] Each of these signs is a combination of six lines, which are either divided or undivided. The undivided lines signify the positive, light, male, heavenly pole; the divided lines, the corresponding negative pole. According to the manner in which each sign is composed of a varying combination of positive and negative lines, the total character of the situation which is represented by the sign is deduced. Each of these sixty-four signs has its own name, through which the character of the situation is indicated.[2] Both the signs and their names seem to

[1] *Translators' Note. Achillea millefolium.* See pp. 109-111.

[2] *Translators' Note.* Wilhelm was deeply interested in the *Book of Changes*, and began to print his explanations of them in his

be of great antiquity. According to tradition, King Wên and his son, the Duke of Chou, undertook a rearrangement of this book at the beginning of the Chou period, and added more detailed oracles. This was the Book of Changes of the Chou Dynasty that Confucius had before him.

Tradition also assigns to Confucius a share in this work, by ascribing to him the supplementary commentaries and discussions. This material is

Pekinger Abende, II and III, February-March, 1923, pp. 12 ff. As these *Peking Evenings* were brochures which were printed as manuscript to be sent to friends, a brief excerpt may be of interest. His explanation of the first hexagram, for example, which is composed of six unbroken lines, goes into greater detail than Legge's (*Sacred Books of the East*, Vol. XVI.) Each of the six lines of each hexagram has, in Chinese, its own interpretation. The Chinese interpretation of the last of the six lines of the first hexagram is thus translated by Legge: "In the sixth (or topmost) line, undivided (we see its subject as) the dragon exceeding the proper limits. There will be occasion for repentance." Wilhelm, after his translation of the Chinese, adds his own interpretation, as follows: "If one wishes to mount so high that one loses touch with the rest of mankind, one is left lonely, and that necessarily leads to failure. In this there lies a warning against titanic upward striving which goes beyond one's strength. A crash to the depths would be the result." (*Pekinger Abende*, II, III, p. 16.) This first, or Chien, hexagram has the form: ☰ . See, also, bibliography, *sub I Ging*.

added to the work in the form of the so-called Ten Wings. They are: (1) and (2) Commentary on the Implications of the Signs as a Whole,[1] (3) Commentary on the "Pictures" that are Represented by the Signs, (4) Commentary on the Words Added to the Individual Lines, (5) and (6) The Great Essay, a Connected Philosophical Discourse, (7) An Exhaustive Commentary on the First Two Signs, (8) A Discussion of the Eight Fundamental Signs,[2] (9) The Order of the Sixty-four Signs, (10) Miscellaneous Definitions of the Names of the Signs.

There is no doubt that this material, part of which is in considerable disorder, is of very uneven value. Numbers 4, 9, and 10 are of very slight worth, while other portions are extremely interesting. But no portion of the work can, with any degree of certainty, be traced to Confucius,

[1] *Translator's Note.* Traditionally attributed in part to King Wên. See Legge, *Sacred Books of the East,* Vol. XVI, Introduction.

[2] *Translators' Note.* The eight signs are the so-called *pa kua,* which are referred to in English as the *eight trigrams,* and which are a favorite motif in Chinese art. They follow: (1) ☰; (2) ☷; (3) ☳; (4) ☶; (5) ☲; (6) ☵; (7) ☱; (8) ☴.

even though the Commentaries on the Implications and on the Pictures may, perhaps, be ascribed
to him. At all events, Sse-Ma Ch'ien does not as-
sume that Confucius wrote any part of the I
Ching. To be sure, Confucius gave his disciples
orally partial explanations, which were very interesting and detailed, for the signs and lines of the
book, as they are found in Number 7, for the first
two signs, and in various parts of Numbers 5 and
6 for individual lines of other parts as well. These
statements seem to represent a stratum of tradition
which does not trace back very far beyond Confucius. Unfortunately, if such a commentary on all
the signs might have existed, only scattered fragments of it are now extant. Nevertheless, the Book
of Changes contains a great mass of Chinese
wisdom, and for this reason it deserves to be
brought far more to the attention of those who
wish to study Chinese thought than has here-
tofore been the case. A special movement has
taken place latterly in the Confucian School
which has applied itself particularly to the Book
of Changes.

e. *The Spring and Autumn Annals*

According to tradition, Confucius wrote the Spring and Autumn Annals in his extreme old age, after his final return to his native state from his wanderings. In the entire older literature, we find this work mentioned with the greatest respect. Not only the Confucianist, Mencius, speaks of it as of a royal work. The Taoist writer, Chuang Chou, speaks of it in terms of the highest admiration. And Confucius himself was conscious that the love and hate of posterity would be accorded him on the basis of this work.

If we compare the book which has been handed down to us as the Spring and Autumn Annals, and which lays claim to being the work that is the object of all this praise, with those judgments of value according to which the work must surely be the most significant from the hand of the Master, we are, as Occidentals, at first view most bitterly disappointed. The book is neither more nor less than a barren chronicle, in briefest lapidary style, without pragmatic detailed explanations, without theoretical judgments: year by year, the events are reckoned and an eclipse of the sun or a plague of grasshoppers has quite as much emphasis as a regicide or an imperial hunting expedition. It is no wonder that, for a long time, no one in Europe had any notion how to treat the work; indeed, that some people even arrived at the conclusion that the actual work of Confucius was contained in the document that, under the name of the Tso Chuan, passed as a commentary on the Annals of Confucius by a certain Tso-Ch'iu Ming.[1]

Upon closer examination, the above position has proved untenable. Since the work of the Chinese scholar, K'ang Yu-wei, it can be regarded as conclusively proved that the Tso Chuan and the so-called Conversations of the States (Kuo Yü) originally formed one connected work, which was not written in annalistic arrangement, and which, centuries later, in Han times, was divided up by the librarian, Liu Hsin, and rearranged as a commentary on the Spring and Autumn Annals.[2]

[1] Cf. Grube's discussion in his *History of Chinese Literature. Translators' Note.* Wilhelm Grube, *Geschichte der chinesischen Litteratur,* 2te Ausgabe, Leipzig, 1909. Pp. 68 ff., p. 70 cit.

[2] Cf. O. Franke, by whom the investigations of K'ang Yu-wei have been made accessible to European readers.

The relationships become clearer to us when we take into consideration a statement of Confucius himself which is handed down to us regarding this work: "The facts are from the time of the Princes Huan, of Ch'i, and Wên, of Chin; the style is historical, but I have taken the liberty of determining the sense myself." In point of fact, the Spring and Autumn Annals were probably, in their origin, the official annals of Confucius' native country, the State of Lu. He makes these annals the basis of his labour throughout. And actually what he does is only to make the expressions specific and exact. Through this use of specific and exact expressions, we can deduce the judgment which Confucius passes on events. Some examples may make this clear. In the period discussed in the Annals, a great number of regicides occurred. But there is a decided difference in the manner in which they are recorded.

In one place, we read: "The people of Wei killed Chou Yü." In another place: "Shang Ch'ên, the Crown Prince of Ch'u, murdered his prince." Or: "Chao Tun murdered his prince." Through this variety of terms, by which Confucius corrected the original text, the measure of guilt is determined. In the first case, for example, the entire guilt is ascribed to the prince. Hence, he is not designated as prince, and is not "murdered," but "killed." It is the people of Wei who killed him. His death, then, is represented as a just punishment, carried out by the people. Indeed, the prince in question was an evil and a cruel ruler, who richly deserved his fate. The second case is exactly the opposite. Here the Crown Prince is expressly designated by name as the murderer, so that the double guilt of regicide and parricide descends upon him. The third case is still different. Chao Tun was a minister. He was obliged to leave the court on account of intrigues. Even before he crossed the border, a kinsman of his killed the prince out of revenge. Chao Tun returned and left the murder unpunished; therefore the guilt is attributed by Confucius to him.

Thus Confucius has secretly introduced into the text, which is seemingly so harmless, a strict historical judgment for the initiated who understand the connection. He has, however, taken care that this connection should not be unrecognized. In his oral instruction he gave his pupils the explanation of the text-determinations. There are two existent commentaries to the work, by Kung Yang and Ku Liang, which were composed on the basis of these oral statements of the Master, and which explain why he altered the text when he did, and what moral judgment is intended through this correction of the text.

Because of this, the effect of this work was really enormous. As Mencius remarks, it was so great that rebellious sons and treacherous officials became terrified. And Ch'in Shih Huang Ti felt such terror of this work that his burning of the books may be said to have been directed, first of all, against it. But the "First Emperor" did not get rid of it by these means. It has remained an incorruptible codex of political morality throughout the centuries and has had such an effect that Chinese statesmen, even when they departed from its teachings, were yet never able to avoid a silent reckoning with its judgments. Thus Confucius actually proved himself the uncrowned king through this quiet labour of an author and a teacher.

THE POST-CONFUCIAN WRITINGS

a. *The Conversations of Confucius* (*Lun Yü*)

This work is, at the present time, quite correctly considered the most direct and reliable source which we have for Confucius, his life, and his doctrines. It is not, of course, a product of Confucius, nor yet—at least, as it is now formulated—of his immediate disciples, who, in part, also appear as "Masters." But it may safely be assumed that data or traditions regarding the "Master" form the sources of the work, and that these were given their final form by the next succeeding generation. This material has a double tradition: the one, in Lu, the native state of the Master, which may, in general, be accepted as closer to the original; and the other, in the neighbouring state of Ch'i. In the Han Dynasty, these two sources were united by Chêng K'ang-Ch'êng, in the opus known today as the Lun Yü. The contents of this book are, for the most part, short aphorisms introduced by the words, "The Master spake." Often the occasion for the word of the Master is also given in a sentence. The later portions of the book offer, in part, actual brief conversations with pupils or opponents, often surrounded by a framework of narrative. All in all, we have before us in this collection solid, reliable material, which must always be taken into primary consideration in any presentation of the doctrines of Confucius.

b. *School Conversations* (*Chia Yü*)

The School Conversations, which contain a rich collection of anecdotes, conversations, and reports, would offer a welcome supplement to the Analects (Lun Yü), limited as the latter are to sententiae, if they could be used with the same confidence as the Lun Yü. Now it is fairly certain that a work with the title School Conversations [1] actually existed at the time of the burning of the books by Ch'in Shih Huang Ti, and also that it was subsequently rediscovered. But no one knows what has become of this work. What we have today under

---

[1] *Translators' Note.* The word *chia*, which literally means *family*, is here used as it is in the expression *ju chia*, which means *Confucian School*. The term *Chia Yü*, therefore, is somewhat similar to *table talk*.

this name was certainly not published until the beginning of the third century A.D., by Wang Su; and it is supposed that it was also written by him. At all events, it contains passages which can be paralleled—usually with some frequency—elsewhere in post-Confucian literature, and, in part, it consists of a recension which is superior to the other recensions of the passages in question. It is probably best to postulate, as a later stratum after the Analects, a tradition of fairly large anecdotal portions from the life of Confucius, which were handed down in the various Confucian school-groups as tradition, and which found their way into the contemporary literature of the Ch'in and Han periods. This later stratum of tradition was perhaps the product of imperceptible stages, since the various strata of the text of the Lun Yü lead to the conclusion that there was a further development in the course of time. After having investigated the Chia Yü, and after having established the fact that practically the entire material has parallels elsewhere, I came to the conclusion that the Chia Yü does not deserve to be ranked as an original work, but should rather be considered a

valuable collection of then current material, one
of the direct or indirect sources of which may
have been the ancient Chia Yü. The Chia Yü,
then, can naturally not claim the same authority as
the Lun Yü, but they represent a later stage of
the tradition.

c. *The Great Learning (Ta Hsüeh), Measure and
Mean (Chung Yung), and the Book of
Reverence (Hsiao Ching)*[1]

Besides the Analects (Lun Yü) and the writ-
ings of the philosopher Mencius, two thin bro-
chures belong among those writings which were
collected in the Sung Dynasty as a sort of New
Testament. These two brief works are The Great
Learning (Ta Hsüeh) and The Doctrine of the
Mean (Chung Yung). They are also found in the
Li Chi, a collection of Notes Concerning Man-

[1] *Translators' Note.* The usual appellations of these three
works are: *The Great Learning, The Doctrine of the Mean,* and
The Classic of Filial Piety. These English names are used by
the translators. Ku Hung Ming and numerous other Chinese
scholars strongly object to Legge's translation: *The Great Learning.* Some of them have tried to introduce the phrase from
Newman: *The Idea of a University.*

ners which dates from the Han Dynasty, and which has already been mentioned. Sse-Ma Ch'ien states that The Doctrine of the Mean is the composition of Tze Sse, the grandson of the Master.[1] Chu Hsi, who lived in the Sung period, analyzes the Great Learning into a text, which he traces back to Confucius, and a commentary, which the disciple Tsêng Tze is said to have written. Only this much is to be said concerning the form of the text, as edited by Chu Hsi: that he has, in a somewhat arbitrary fashion, made something entirely new out of the ancient works. Nor does he disclose whence he has the tradition regarding the authorship of the Great Learning. Suspicions can, therefore, not be suppressed, and we must rely chiefly upon internal evidence in including these two brief works in a history of Chinese literature.[2] The attempt has recently been made to represent them as the fruit of a combination of Taoistic and Confucianistic teachings, and to seek for the time

[1] *Translators' Note.* Cf. Giles, No. 1040, where his cognomen is given as Chi and his style, or appellation, as Tze Sse.

[2] *Translators' Note.* That is, to class them as pure literature rather than as philosophy.

of their composition beyond the philosopher Mencius down into the time of the Ch'in Dynasty. This hypothesis, is, however, not probable, since the accepted Confucian canon of the Ch'in Dynasty was that of the philosopher Hsün Ch'ing, which is based upon a pessimistic interpretation of human nature as originally evil.[1] This philosophical trend contradicts the two tractates in question. We should, accordingly, be obliged either to proceed further down into the Han period— and this is inadvisable for other reasons—or to continue in the traditionally accepted opinion that the two works represent a transition between the period of the Analects (Lun Yü) and of Mencius. After consideration of the questions involved, this seems to me to be the safest standpoint; in which case it is in all probability necessary to place the Great Learning even earlier than the Doctrine of the Mean.[2]

[1] Both Li Ssu, the all-powerful Minister of Ch'in, and his friend, Han Fei, were pupils of Hsün Ch'ing.

Translators' Note. Cf. Giles, No. 807, under Hsün K'uang.

[2] Hu Shih, in his *History of Chinese Philosophy*, also retains this system of dating, in spite of the proposals of Ts'ai Yüan P'ei for a later date.

It is quite probable that the Classic of Filial Piety (Hsiao Ching) was not composed by the pupil of Confucius, Tsêng Shên.[1] On the other hand, it is already mentioned in the paralipomena to Mencius; and it contains no doctrines which could not be joined to those of the older period.

d. *The Philosopher Mencius* [2]

The works of the philosopher Mencius form the fourth book which Chu Hsi published in the Sung period, together with the Analects of Confucius, the Great Learning, and the Doctrine of the Mean, as the Four Sacred Books—along with the above-named Five Classical Writings. This book is in excellent textual condition and may be regarded as a perfect reproduction of the teachings of Mencius, who lived from 372 to 289 B.C. Mencius is the most significant representative of the philosophic school, which dates from the disciple, Tsêng Shên, via the grandson of the Master, Tse Sse, and which is generally regarded as the

---

[1] *Translators' Note.* Cf. Giles, No. 2022, under Tsêng Tsan.

[2] *Translators' Note.* As Wilhelm always uses the transliteration of the Chinese name of Confucius (K'ung Tse), he does the same for Mencius (Mong K'o).

most orthodox school. The picture which is drawn in this work of the life and the doctrines of Confucius is in practical harmony with that which we gain from the other sources of first rank. We may, therefore, accept this book as a perfectly valid testimony for the Confucian doctrine. In many respects it follows the main ideas of Confucius down to minute details, and seeks to give them a psychological foundation, and to round them out psychologically. To be sure, it cannot be denied that, with the development and rationalization of the doctrines of the Master, a certain resultant shallowness and one-sidedness were unavoidable. Whereas Confucius was the practical statesman, who gives positive expression to his doctrines and who seeks to make them effective among his disciples through the influence of his powerful personality, Mencius is the clever debater who tries to confute and always to be in the right in his duels with other schools of philosophy, but who, for the sake of greater clarity, on the other hand, reinterprets certain of the basic ideas of the Master, such as his conception of humanity and of love in the highest sense, by juxtaposing justice and duty to love, when actually the two together, love and duty, indicate the highest ideal. Mencius' ideas about music were also, for instance, much more superficial than those of Confucius, and it would be easy to find other similar examples. But all this does not merit attention when compared with the great passion and the great courage with which Mencius entered the lists for the true and the good in the Confucian sense; and it was surely due in large measure to him that other hostile movements lost in influence, and that the influence of Confucius was strengthened.

e. *The Philosopher Hsün Ch'ing*

Somewhat later than Mencius lived his great rival within the school of Confucius, Hsün Ch'ing, the dates of whose birth and death cannot be determined with exactitude. It is probable that he died about the year 213 B.C., and certainly at a very advanced age.

In contrast to Mencius, whom he condemns for having taught the original goodness of the human race, Hsün Tze adheres to the standpoint that man is by nature originally evil, and that he becomes good, so to speak, artificially, only through civilization.[1] Hsün Tze sees manners as the means for this compulsory reformation of humanity, and manners also play an important rôle with Confucius himself. But with Confucius manners are a mild force, which start from the convincing personal power of a great personality and are expanded like an organic growth, while Hsün Ch'ing sees in manners, in the first instance, the fixed form which must achieve its aims and reconstruct man with the coercive power of a law. It is at this point that Hsün Ch'ing deviates widely from the very core of the Confucian doctrines. He is, however, still near enough in time to the earliest period of Confucianism to be reckoned as a proof of the earlier form of the doctrine.

With Hsün Ch'ing, the classical period of Confucianism is terminated. There follow the historical destinies of Confucianism and its conflicts with other times and other cultural conditions.

[1] *Translators' Note. The Trimetrical Classic,* a book written in lines of three characters (ideograms) each, which for centuries was the first work placed in the hands of the Chinese school child, begins, "Man's nature is originally good." Hsün Ch'ing is usually referred to in English as Hsün Tze.

Chapter IV

THE TEACHINGS OF CONFUCIUS

ACCORDING TO THE DATA OF THE PUPILS

Conversations, The Great Learning, The Doctrine of the Mean

IF WE seek the central concept which crystallizes the doctrines of Confucius in the oldest sources, we find the idea of mankind, humanity, humanitarianism, kindness, morality, or however we choose to translate the expression "jen." It is characteristic that the word "jen," *humanitarianism,* is also closely connected in the Chinese with the word "jen," *man.* It is written with the ideograms for "man" (*human being*) and "two," and thus designates the relationship of two or more human beings to each other.[1] Considering the type of works in which the views of Confucius are

---

[1] *Translators' Note.* In Wilhelm's translation of the Lun Yü, he translates this "jen" (仁) either as *Sittlichkeit* or *Liebe* (*morality* or *love*). In his translation of Mencius, he more frequently uses *Liebe.* A usual English translation has been *benevolence,* but the type of love is that represented by the Greek *agape* (ἀγάπη).

handed down, we cannot expect connected discussions, but merely scattered aphorisms. These, however, are rounded out to make a unified picture.

Humanitarianism is that which is intrinsic and original in the very nature of man. It is the gift of nature, the spirit, which man has received in order to live. It is, therefore, something which is not far removed from any individual. As soon as one wishes it, it is present for him, and it is not difficult to realize. Let the will but be unified, and the will can bring it about. Humanitarianism expresses itself in a love for all mankind which corresponds to the relationships in which one stands to mankind. Its root is filial piety. Beginning with the natural feelings of affection within the family, it mounts to the differentiated relationships of duty in state and society.

Humanitarianism expresses itself in forms and ceremonials (*li*). Such forms and ceremonials are not merely custom and practice, but they are the correct expression of a corresponding inner attitude. All forms without the basic truth of inner attitude are empty and despicable. For Confucius, indeed, this inner attitude transcends in importance the perfection of external form. The newness of his doctrines lies in this very point; they strive to create a consciousness in each individual of the great laws of form, and are, in this respect, related to the teachings of the Hebrew prophets. Thus, for Confucius, beautiful manners are the correct expression for beautiful inner impulses. Correct form is, therefore, something which, in its very fundamentals, is artistic. For Confucius, therefore, good manners and music are closely allied. Decorum rules conduct, music rules the emotions. And a harmonious emotion is an ineluctable presupposition for form. This humanity is shown in the fact that its starting-point is an unconditioned sincerity toward itself. Only if one does not lie to oneself can one hope to be master of one's own mistakes and weaknesses, which can be perceived in the mirror of others. What is necessary is not a theoretical knowledge for its own sake, but a practical exercise in and from communion with other men. The presupposition of learning is constant practice. Thus one arrives at correct inner feelings. It is at this point that the individual is inseparably

connected with the universal. One can draw conclusions about others from oneself. What one does
not wish for oneself, one ought not to do to any
one else; what one recognizes as desirable for oneself one ought to be willing to grant to others.
This contact with the universally human element
at the bottom of one's own soul (*shu*), and the
corresponding action (*chung*)—this is the one
connecting thread in the teaching of the Master.

Humanitarianism is not incorporated in each
individual with equal clarity. There are saints and
philosophers who have it from birth: they are the
great heroes and civilizers of mankind; there are,
on the other hand, dolts and fools who seem almost
incorrigible. But by nature people are close to each
other. The way to the goal is open to all—whether
one man reaches it almost without trying, by following his natural talents; whether another man
strives for it, making it a part of himself through
learning; or, finally, whether a third man must
struggle and wrestle and again and again gather
himself together—when once the goal is reached,
it is the same for all. Therefore Confucius sub-

stitutes for the old differences in rank between people a new relationship: the difference between the noble man, who affirms his duty for its own sake, absorbing in free autonomy the divinity into his own volition, and the man of no ability, the common man, who, actuated by external motives, lives in fear and hope, who can only be led, and who does not progress through inner knowledge. Thus the noble are destined to lead and the commoners to be led.

It is the wish of Confucius to educate dominant personalities, who develop within themselves the force of their own individuality, through which they can influence others. For only that which is entirely true in one's own life has the power to change others. Mere words, mere external means, such as laws and punishments, accomplish only external submission, with secret resistance, but do not attain any inner—that is, real—success.

For Confucius, the management of this force, its starting-point in society, is made feasible by means of an organization of society. For him, human society is not a mechanism, but a living organism, in which an active effectiveness of forces is possible. The nucleus is the family, within which natural feelings of affection need only to be regulated and properly directed. Beyond this is the state, in which what in the family is love becomes duty. The next step, then, is *mankind.* For in Confucius' way of thinking it is the humanity within each individual which, in the last analysis, is just as much a reality as is mankind. And the absolute necessity for the realization of his ideal is the conviction that all men are brothers.

ACCORDING TO THE SPRING AND AUTUMN ANNALS AND THE BOOK OF CHANGES

The Spring and Autumn Annals are in one place designated by Mencius as a regal book. Here we find the method through which Confucius sought to regulate the world. The key to this method is also given in one passage of the Conversations. A disciple, on one occasion, asks Confucius what he would consider the most important thing if he were entrusted with the government of a state, and he answers: *the rectification of the names.* Here we have to deal with a remarkable trend of thought, which, however, is very important if we expect to understand Confucius' concept of the creation of civilization and of reform.

For Confucius, names are not mere abstractions, but they signify something ideally co-ordinated with actuality. To each object, the name comes as the *designation of its being*. And if an object is correctly named, something essential is contained in the name regarding the nature of this object. The totality of these names—for Confucius, it is here primarily a question of designations in human society—forms in itself a connected system. And a name is evaluated according to the position which it occupies in this system as a designation. If one then compares the ideal and therefore correct names with reality, one can at once recognize whether the name fits the conditions or not. In the designation and in its application to a set of facts, there exists at once a judgment of value, determined concerning this set of facts. For example, if I apply the name "father" to a person who is actually paternally affectionate, or the name "son" to one who is actually reverential, there lies in this nomenclature a strong element of approval;

the relationship appears normal. Where, on the other hand, reality does not coincide with the values contained in the name, the name is not attributed to the *de facto* ruler. A father who is not paternal does not deserve the name "father"; a son without reverence does not at all deserve the name "son." To illustrate this, Confucius wrote, in the Spring and Autumn Annals, a story from the epoch which preceded his own, in which he always chooses the designations which correspond to the true state of affairs. If, for example, the Son of Heaven is fetched to a gathering of allies and is obliged to come whether he wishes to or not, there is in this situation something unworthy and unseemly which does not correspond to the dignity of the Son of Heaven. Confucius uses, therefore, for that event, the designation: "The Son of Heaven betook himself to the south in order to hunt." For if the Son of Heaven comes to an assembly of princes, this action can naturally arise only from his own initiative. A contrary situation is thus criticized by means of the above designation, and is branded as wrong. In this fashion, Confucius exercised, in his Spring and Autumn Annals, a systematic criticism of social conditions in the preceding centuries.[1]

The decisive feature in this systematic criticism is that we here have before us a philosophic attitude which recalls Plato's doctrine of ideas, except for the fact that the whole concept is given a practical turn. With Plato, ideas are the eternal images of actual terrestrial objects. These objects have a share in the idea, and the scale of values is measured according to this share in the idea. For Confucius, it is a question of recognizing the true names, not only to measure reality by them, but also to be able to reform reality.

But how can reality be formed? The answer to this query is obtained if we adduce the fundamental thought expressed by Confucius in connection with the Book of Changes. The Book of Changes rests upon the assumption that all earthly happenings are in a constant state of flux, like the

[1] *Translators' Note.* This Rectification of the Names (*Chêng Ming*) is one of the most important factors in Chinese life, even at the present time. It accounts for the wholesale change of names accompanying dynastic changes, and is, for example, at the basis of the modern name for Peking: Peiping (= *Pei P'ing, northern peace*). Chinese history since the 1910 Revolution would furnish numerous examples. See p. 51.

water of a stream, which flows on, day and night, without ceasing. The individual conditions are developed from imperceptible, germlike beginnings. They then enter into the full effectiveness of their forces, in order, in the end, to pass gradually over into other conditions, after they have exhausted their forces. Now if one can recognize the nuclei, one can succeed in influencing events by giving an imperceptible direction which will lead to the wished-for goal of this development. If one wished to affect immediately the conditions which are in a state of development, at most an effect would result, representative of an accommodation of the circumstances to be affected to the effecting force; that is to say, an effect not corresponding with the goal. This, for example, is the reason why Confucius opposes the method of regulating the state by means of laws and punishments: that is to say, by means of force. The effect of such a system will only be an evasion on the part of the people, and a condition of universal hypocrisy. If, on the other hand, one works upon the manners of the people by means of the power of a direct influence, the evil influences are smothered in the germ before they have any chance whatsoever to express themselves, and the goal is reached. Herein lies the deeper philosophical foundation for the strong emphasis on decorum and music in popular education, and for the rejection of external means of punishment.

At this point, Confucius and his ideas are in close proximity to those of Lao Tze, just as the Book of Changes may be regarded as the common foundation for the doctrines of both. The only difference is this: that Lao Tze regards the development of mankind to consciously intellectual life and to social and political organization as mis-development, and, for his part, leads mankind away from the whole realm of phenomena into the metaphysical—the other-worldly. Confucius, on the other hand, affirms the development of culture as such. His striving is only to preserve this development from becoming mechanically superficial and chaotically confused in its ideas of right and wrong and thereby to keep it supple and adaptable to the demands of the age and of the locality. Just here lies the element of universality in the doctrine of Confucius. Although historically conditioned in his individual stamp through the situation at the end of the period of Chinese feudalism, his doctrines contain certain fundaments which can be applied in every age and place. And thus it is no wonder that his teaching possessed the power of proving itself a suitable foundation for Chinese religion and philosophy many centuries later, when the establishment of the *imperium* had long since swept away the feudal system. And, up to the present time, this doctrine has survived every change of conditions. Temporarily forced into the background by other influences, especially by Buddhism, which, during the median periods of Chinese history, attracted the entire interest of the spiritually minded in China, Confucianism has again and again assimilated the foreign elements, and, itself rejuvenated and transformed, yet always the same within, has mounted to the light of day.

The most difficult test of Confucianism must be met in the present. For the European-Occidental civilization which has so irresistibly penetrated China is, of course, the most powerful enemy that Confucianism has ever encountered. To begin

with, it seems as though the old Confucian doctrine, after having been compelled to retreat step
by step, had now finally been disposed of. But the
last word has not yet been spoken. Confucianism,
as such, very definitely possesses sufficient inner
elasticity to accommodate itself also to modern
conditions. To be sure, the attempt which was
made, in the few years since the establishment of
the Chinese Republic, to compete effectively with
Christianity by means of a Confucian state church,
was bound to fail, for it signified a merely external
taking over of ecclesiastical forms which are already under fire even in their own home-lands and
which do not correspond to the spirit of Confucianism. For Confucianism is community of doctrine,
but not ecclesiasticism. Therefore it was at no time
ruled by a dogma promulgated by a majority; on
the contrary, a variety of tendencies and opinions
existed side by side. The failure of the new Confucian church in China proves, however, nothing
in regard to the final fate of Confucianism. In the
last analysis, it will be a question of finding people
who grasp these doctrines in their essential depth,
and of finding new forms with which to make the

old content alive. Certainly a new form means, at the same time, a reforming of the content. Form and content are, in a certain sense, one, and cannot be kept mechanically apart. Thus the Reform-Confucianism of the Sung period is not merely a mechanical renovation of the old, classical Confucianism. And the idealistic-magic doctrine of Wang Yang-ming, in the Ming period, is again a recasting.[1] If a reawakening of Confucianism ensues today, this reawakening will once more signify a new stage of development for Confucianism. But just here lies the secret of Confucius. As he naïvely took over Chinese antiquity and did nothing more than inspire it with a new motivation, just so his influence has again and again been that of offering a new dynamic. And this spiritual impulse which he represented may, in all probability, have still further effect at the present time. It is only a question of the right people.

For *truth cannot make men great, but men must make truth great. It is not truth which regulates the world, but man must take the place of truth; then the world will be regulated.*

[1] *Translators' Note.* Cf. F. G. Henke, *The Philosophy of Wang Yang Ming.* Chicago, 1917.

Chapter V

SPECIMENS OF THE TEXT

FROM THE CONVERSATIONS OF CONFUCIUS
(LUN YÜ)

THE Master said: "If one guides by means of decrees, and regulates by means of punishments, the people evade and have no conscience. If one guides through the force of personality and through morals, the people have conscience, and attain the good" (II, 3).[1]

The Master said, "Wisdom frees from doubts, morality frees from suffering, determination frees from fear" (IX, 28).

Yen Yüan asked Confucius concerning the essence of morality. The Master replied: "It is by conquering oneself and by devoting oneself to the laws of beauty that one accomplishes morality. The whole world would turn to morality, if it would, for one day, conquer itself and devote itself

[1] *Translators' Note.* What Wilhelm translates as *Gewissen* (*conscience*) has the ordinary meaning of *shame*, and is thus translated by Legge. What Wilhelm translates as *Kraft des Wesens* (*force of personality*), Legge translates by *virtue.*

157

to the laws of beauty. To accomplish morality depends upon each individual, or does it perhaps depend upon others?"

Yen Yüan said, "May I ask for the single steps in the process?"

The Master answered: "What does not correspond to the law of beauty, *that* you must not regard; what does not correspond to the law of beauty, *that* you must not heed; what does not correspond to the ideal of beauty, *that* you must not discuss; what does not correspond to the ideal of beauty, *that* you must not do."

Yen Yüan said, "Although my power is but weak, yet will I strongly endeavour to act in accordance with this dictum" (XII, 1).[1]

Baron Chi K'ang asked Master K'ung concerning the essence of government. Master K'ung replied: "To rule means to make right. If Your Highness takes over the government in a spirit of right being, who would dare not to be right?" (XII, 17.)

---

[1] *Translators' Note.* Wilhelm's use of the word *Schönheit* (*beauty*) is extremely interesting. The Chinese word *li* is usually translated *propriety*, and is thus interpreted by Legge.

Baron Chi K'ang asked Master K'ung concerning the essence of government, and said: "If one kills criminals in order to help those who walk on the right path, how would that be?" Master K'ung countered with this reply: "If Your Highness carries on the government, what need have you for killing? If Your Highness desires that which is good, the people will become good. The character of the ruler is the wind; the character of the common people is the grass. The grass must bend when the wind blows over it" (XII, 19).

Fan Ch'ih walked with the Master under the Rain Altar. He said, "May I ask how one can exalt one's character, correct one's secret faults, and distinguish that which is unclear?" The Master replied: "That is a good question! First the labour, then the enjoyment: is not character elevated thereby? Fighting against one's sins, and not fighting against the sins of others: are not secret faults corrected thereby? Forgetting one's own person and involving one's relatives in difficulties for the sake of a morning's anger: is not that a case of unclearness?" (XII, 21.)

Tze Chang asked concerning the conditions for

159

advancement. The Master replied: "To be conscientious and true in one's speech, to be reliable
and careful in one's actions, and even if one dwells
among the barbarians of the South or the North:
one will thus advance. But if one is not conscientious and true in one's speech, and if one is not
reliable and careful in one's actions, even if one
remains in one's native environment—can one at
all advance thus? When one is standing, let him
see these things as though they were a two-horse
chariot before him; when one is sitting in a chariot,
let him see them like the side walls beside him.
In this manner, one will advance." Tze Chang
wrote this down upon his girdle (XV, 5).

Yen Yüan asked concerning the basic principles
for the governing of a country. The Master replied: "Follow the division of time of the Hsia
Dynasty, ride in the chariot of state of the Yin
Dynasty, wear the ceremonial head-covering of
the Chou Dynasty. As far as music is concerned,
take the Shao music, with its rhythmic pantomimes.
Forbid the sound of the Chêng music, and keep
eloquent people at a distance; for the sound of

the Chêng music is licentious, and eloquent people are dangerous" (XV, 10).

Master K'ung said: "When the world is in order, civilization and art, wars and punitive military expeditions, proceed from the Son of Heaven. If the world is not in order, civilization and art, wars and punitive military expeditions, proceed from the feudal princes. When these things proceed from the feudal princes, it is seldom a longer period than ten generations until the princes have lost their power. When these things proceed from the nobles, it is seldom a longer period than five generations until the nobles have lost their power. When the vassals forcibly take to themselves the power in the empire, it is seldom a longer period than three generations until they have lost it.

"When the world is in order, the guidance is not in the hands of the nobles. When the world is in order, there is no discussion of the state of affairs among the masses" (XVI, 2).[1]

Master K'ung said: "The Sage has a holy awe

[1] *Translators' Note.* Under the Empire, there was a sign in public places: *Wu t'an kuo shih* (*Do not discuss public affairs*).

of three things: He stands in awe of the will of God; he stands in awe of great men; he stands in awe of the words of the holy men of antiquity. The common man does not know the will of God. He does not stand in awe of Him; he is disrespectful to great men, and he mocks the words of the saints" (XVI, 8).

FROM THE GREAT LEARNING (TA HSÜEH)

The Foundations

The way of the Great Learning consists in the clarification of originally clear predispositions, in the love of mankind, and in resting in the highest excellence (I).

If one understands this resting, then only does one have fixity of purpose. If one has fixity of purpose, then only can one succeed in being tranquil. If one is tranquil, then only can one succeed in finding peace. If one has peace, then only is one able to reflect. Only after reflection can one succeed in obtaining what one wishes (II).

Things have their stock and ramification; actions have end and beginning. If one understands what comes first and what follows, one approaches the right path (III).

Since the ancients wished to clarify the original predispositions in the world, they first ordered their own territory; for the purpose of ordering their own territory, they first regulated their house; for the purpose of regulating their house, they first ennobled their own lives; for the purpose of ennobling their own lives, they strove to attain the right attitude of mind; for the purpose of attaining the right attitude of mind, they strove for sincerity in their thoughts; for the purpose of obtaining sincere thoughts, they strove for complete knowledge; complete knowledge rests upon the understanding of actuality (IV).[1]

Only through grasp of actuality does one attain

---

[1] *Translators' Note.* This section contains extremely interesting examples, not only of the Chinese ability to balance thoughts in gnomic utterance, but also of the peculiarity of the Chinese language, which permits the use of the same ideogram, not only in a different sense, but also as a different part of speech. Wilhelm translates *die ursprünglichen Anlagen läutern,* using the word *Anlage,* which means *tendency, predisposition,* to translate the first *ming* and using *läutern* to translate the second *ming* of the Chinese *tsai ming ming tê.* Legge renders the phrase: *to illustrate illustrious virtue.* The usual translation of *ming* is *bright.*

to complete knowledge; only through complete knowledge do thoughts become sincere; only through sincere thoughts does one attain to the right state of mind; only the right state of mind makes possible the ennobling of life; only through the ennobling of one's own life does the regulation of one's family become possible; only through the regulation of the family does the ordering of the country become possible; only through the ordering of the individual states does peace upon earth become possible (V).

From the supreme ruler of the world down to the man of the people the same thing holds: for all, the ennobling of the individual life is the stem. That any one, in spite of the fact that the stem in his case is in disorder, might be able to bring the ramifications into correct order—*that* cannot be done. If any one has an indifferent attitude toward that which is nearest to him, it is impossible for him to regard that which is more remote as important. This is the basis of knowledge. The recognition of the basis is the only thing which might be called complete knowledge (VI).

FROM THE DOCTRINE OF THE MEAN
(CHUNG YUNG)

The will of God in us is called our nature. That which guides our nature is called the Way. What makes the Way possible is education. One must not for a moment depart from this Way. Anything from which one may depart, that is not the Way.

For this reason, the superior man is cautious and careful, even when he sees nothing; and he is afraid and a-tremble, even when he hears nothing. There is nothing more revealed than the hidden, and nothing more mighty than the invisible. Therefore man keeps watch over his most secret thoughts.

At the point where the feelings of pleasure and displeasure, of sadness and joy, have not yet made their appearance, at that point is the germ of our spiritual being. Where these feelings express themselves and all strike the correct rhythm, at that point is the state of harmonious motion. That spiritual germ is the great root of all being. This harmonious motion is the only path in the world which leads to the goal. If the spiritual germ and the harmonious motion are realized, heaven and earth are in order, and all beings are developed (I).

Chung Ni (Confucius) said: "The superior man lives in measure and moderation, the inferior man lives contrary to measure and moderation. The superior man lives in measure and moderation, for he possesses character and at all times finds moderation. The inferior man lives contrary to measure and moderation, for he is characterless, and knows nothing of which he would be afraid" (II).[1]

The Master said, "Measure and moderation, that is the highest, but for a long time it has been rare to find people who are able to make it an actuality" (III).

The Master said: "I know why no one travels upon the right Way. The Philosophers go beyond

---

[1] *Translators' Note.* Wilhelm's translation, *Mass und Mitte* (literally, *measure and middle*) for *Chung Yung,* is an interesting parallel to the mediaeval German idea of *diu mâze,* which was one of the qualities of the ideal Knight. It is parallel to the Greek *sophrosyne* (σωφροσύνη). Legge translates, *The Doctrine of the Mean.* It is not quite the same as the Latin *aurea mediocriter.*

it, and the fools do not reach it. I know why no one recognizes the right Way. Talented people go beyond it, and those without talent do not reach it.

"Among men there is no one who does not eat and drink, but only the very few know how to appreciate the taste of food" (IV).

The Sage always acts in a manner which corresponds to his position and demands nothing which lies beyond this. If he is in rich and honored circumstances, he leads a life which beseems a man of wealth and honor. If he is in poor and humble circumstances, he leads a life which beseems a man of poverty and low position. If he is among strangers and savages, he leads a life which beseems any one among strangers and savages. If he is in sad or difficult circumstances, he leads a life which beseems any one in need and difficulty. The Sage never finds himself in a situation in which he could not maintain his individuality. In a high position, he makes no demands on those beneath him. In a low position, he has no expectations from those above him. He completes himself and demands nothing of others; thus he remains free from disappointment. He does not murmur against God and complain about mankind.

Thus the Sage lives simply and correctly, and yields himself to the will of God; the people of low standards, however, travel upon dangerous paths in the endeavour to obtain happiness.

The Master said: "The archer has something in common with the Sage. When he misses his aim, he meditates, and seeks the mistake within himself" (XIV).[1]

FROM MENCIUS

King Hui of Liang said: "I really exert myself to the utmost with my kingdom. If there is a crop failure on this side of the Yellow River, I convey a part of the people to the other side, and transport grain to this side. If there is a crop failure in the region on the other side of the river, I act accordingly. If one tests the measures of government of the neighbouring states, one finds no prince who exerts himself as much as I do. And yet the people of the neighbouring kingdoms do

[1] *Translators' Note.* See p. 35. Translators' Note on *chün tze.*

not grow less in number, and my people do not increase. How does that happen?"

Mencius replied: "You, O King, love war. May I use an illustration drawn from war? If the drums roll and weapons cross, and the warriors throw aside their coats of mail, dragging their weapons behind them and running away, the one warrior runs perhaps a distance of a hundred paces and then stands still. Another runs a distance of fifty paces and then stands still. If, now, the one who has run the distance of fifty paces were to laugh at the one who has run a hundred paces, what would you think of that?" The King answered: "That will not do. Although he did not run the full hundred paces, yet he, too, ran away."

Mencius said: "If you, O King, perceive this, you will no longer expect your people to become more numerous than those of the neighbouring states. If one does not lay claim to the peasants' time for other purposes, when these peasants have work to do in the fields, there is so much grain that it cannot all be eaten. If it is forbidden to fish with nets of a narrow mesh in turbid water, there are so many fishes that they cannot all be eaten. If axe and bill enter the forest only at specific times, there is such a quantity of wood and beams that they cannot all be used. If all the grain, the fishes, and the turtles cannot be eaten, if all the wood and beams cannot be used, it is brought to pass that the people nourish the living, inter the ·dead, and no dissatisfaction arises. If the living are nourished, if the dead are interred, if no dissatisfaction arises, that is a beginning which leads to world rule.

"If each homestead of five acres is planted about with mulberry trees, those who are fifty years old can dress themselves in silk. If, in the breeding of chickens, suckling pigs, dogs, and swine, the proper seasons are observed, those who are seventy years old have meat to eat. If from a field of a hundred acres the time necessary for cultivation is not withdrawn, a family of several members will not need to suffer hunger. If one attends carefully to instruction in the schools, and sees to it that the duty of filial and fraternal affection is taught, grey heads and ancients will no longer need to drag loads upon the streets. If those who are seventy years old are dressed in silk and have meat to eat, the young people neither hunger nor freeze, and it is absolutely out of the question that world rule will not come to the prince of that country. If, however, dogs and swine eat that food which should be eaten by human beings, without thought being taken to put a stop to this practice, if people starve to death on the public highways, without thought being taken as to how to help them, and if one still says, in the face of the extinction of the population, 'It is not I who am to blame for this, but the bad year'—this is just the same as if one stabs a person to death and says, 'It is not I who did this, but the sword.' If you, O King, no longer seek to lay the blame on bad years, the people of the entire empire will stream to you" (Bk. I, Part I, Chapter 3).

But he who dwells in the wide house of the world, and who stands in the correct place in the world, and who walks on the straight path in the world, and if he succeeds makes common cause with the people, and if he does not succeed goes his way alone; whom neither riches nor honour can lure, whom neither poverty nor shame can affright, whom neither might nor threats can bend—*he* is a man (Bk. III, Part II, Chapter 3, ¶ 3).[1]

Mencius said: "The compass and the square produce perfect circles and squares. The appointed saints show complete humanity. Whoever wishes, as ruler, to discharge the duties of a ruler, or, as servant, wishes to discharge the duties of a servant, should, in each case, take Yao and Shun as a model. Whoever does not serve his sovereign in the way that Shun served Yao, is one who does not respect his sovereign; whoever does not rule his people in the way that Yao ruled the people, is one who mistreats his people."[2]

Master K'ung said: "There are only two courses: kindness and unkindness, if any one oppresses his people and carries his oppression to the extreme, he brings death upon himself and destruction to his kingdom. If he does not go to the extreme of

[1] *Translators' Note.* This passage is one of the most famous in the Chinese Classics. It is justly admired by the Chinese for its style.

[2] *Translators' Note.* This passage furnishes an excellent example of the way in which the Four Books have become an intrinsic part of the Chinese daily vocabulary. The words *circle* and *square*, *kuei-chü*, are now the regular term for *custom, propriety*. For Yao and Shun, cf. p. 100 and note

oppression, he plunges his life in danger and his kingdom will suffer losses. Posterity will call him the Dark One, the Cruel One, and even if he had filial sons and affectionate grandsons for a hundred generations, they cannot in any way alter this."

This is the significance of what is said in the Book of Odes:

"Yin has his mirror near enough;
  The time of the rulers of Hsia has granted it to
    him" (Book IV, Part I, Chapter 2).

Mencius said: "Whoever mistreats himself cannot be advised. Whoever throws himself away cannot be helped. To disregard order and justice in one's words is what is meant by mistreating oneself; to say, 'I cannot persist in goodness and follow duty' is what is meant by throwing oneself away. Kindness is the tranquil habitation of mankind. Duty is the true path of mankind. Whoever allows this tranquil habitation to stand empty instead of dwelling in it, whoever leaves this true path instead of walking upon it, his case is evil!" (Book IV, Part I, Chapter 10.)

FROM HSÜN CH'ING

When the heart of the Sage is filled to over-flowing, he honours heaven and travels upon the right path. If his heart fails him, he holds to his duty and limits himself. In times of knowledge, he illuminates all the connections of things with his clarity. In times of ignorance, he is upright and simple, and holds to his principles. If he attains a position of influence, he is serious and self-controlled. If he is rejected, he is respectful and seeks to improve himself. In joyful days, he is free and temperate; in sorrowful days, he is calm and regulated. If he has success, he cultivates art and science. If he has no success, he restrains himself and clarifies his principles.

The inferior man does not act thus. If his heart is filled to overflowing, he is impudent and cruel. If his heart fails him, he abandons himself and falls. In times of knowledge, he snatches and steals without ceasing. In times of ignorance, he injures and slays and creates disorder. If he attains a position of influence, he is malicious and proud. If he is rejected, he is vexed and meditates danger for

others. In joyful days, he is frivolous and un-
stable; in sorrowful days, he is excited and without courage. If he has success, he is haughty and
displays favouritism; if he has no success, he
throws himself away and becomes melancholy.
There is an old saying with this significance: The
Sage makes progress in both directions; the inferior man ruins things on every hand (II, 3, 6).

The Sage brings about order. He does not bring
about confusion. What does that mean? Decorum
and justice signify order; that which is not in
harmony with decorum and justice is called confusion. Now the Sage regulates decorum and justice. He does not occupy himself with that which
is contrary to decorum and justice. But if a state
is in confusion, does he not regulate it? Certainly
he regulates a confused state—not, however, by
bringing about confusion and then regulating it,
but by eliminating confusion and replacing it by
order. If a man leads an immoral life, and wishes
to reform, he does not take his immoral actions
and tinker with them, but he removes the immorality, and exchanges it for something better.
Thus he removes the confusion and does not make

futile attempts to regulate it; just as he puts aside immorality and does not tinker with it. What is meant by order is clearly seen in the saying: The Sage occupies himself with order, not with disorder; he occupies himself with improvement, not with immorality (II, 3, 7).

The Sage purifies his conduct, and those who agree with him unite with him. He makes good his words, and he will find words of a similar nature as answer. It is as when a horse neighs; the other horses answer him, not from reason, but because their feelings impel them to do so. If any one has freshly bathed, he shakes out his clothes; if any one has washed his head, he beats out his hat. That is the manner of mankind. Who would wish, if he himself understands a matter perfectly, to seek to learn the foolish chatter of others about it? (II, 3, 8.)

Bibliography

Couvreur, S. J., *Les Quatres Livres avec une Commentaire abrégé en chinois, une double traduction en français et en latin et un vocabulaire des lettres et des noms propres.* Ho kien fu, 1895.

—— *Li Ki.* 2 vols. Ho kien fu, 1913.

Dubs, Homer H., *Hsüntze, The moulder of ancient Confucianism.* London, 1927.

Dvořák, Dr. R., *Chinas Religionen. Erster Teil: Konfuzius und seine Lehre.* Münster i. W., 1895.

Faber, Rev. Ernst, *Confucianism.* Shanghai, American Presbyterian Mission Press, 1895.

Forke, A., *Die Gedankenwelt des chinesischen Kulturkreises. Handbuch der Philosophie.* München und Berlin, 1927.

Franke, O., *Studien zur Geschichte des konfuzianischen Dogmas und der chinesischen Staatsreligion: Das Problem des Tsch'un Ts'iu und Tung Tschungschu's Tsch'un Ts'iu fan lu.* Hamburg, L. Friedrichsen & Co., 1920.

—— *Ueber die chinesische Lehre von den Bezeichnungen. Eine Abhandlung über Lun Yü XIII. 3 und dessen historische Zusammenhänge.* Leyden, 1906.

Gabelentz, Georg von der, *Konfuzius und seine Lehre.* Leipzig, 1888.

Giles, Herbert A., *Religions of Ancient China.* London, 1905.

Grube, Dr. W., *Geschichte der chinesischen Literatur.* Leipzig, 1909.

Hackmann, H., *Chinesische Philosophie.* München, 1927.

de Groot, J. J. M., *Universismus. Die Grundlage der Religion und Ethik des Staatswesens und der Wissenschaften Chinas.* Berlin, 1918.

Hirth, Friedrich, *Confucius and the Chinese.* (*The Unity of Religions*, by Drs. Randall and Smith.) New York, 1910.

Krause, F. E. A., *Ju-Tao-Fo. Die religiösen und philosophischen Systeme Ostasiens.* München, 1924.

Ku Hung Ming, *The Universal Order of Confucius.* London, 1913.

—— *Tzu tsai wên ssu. The Discourses and Sayings of Confucius (Lun-yü).* A new special transl., ill. with quotations from Goethe and other writers. Shanghai, Kelly & Walsh, 1898.

Leang K'i Tsch'ao, *La conception de la Loi et les Théories des Légistes à le veille des Ts'in.* Pekin, 1926.

Legge, James, *The Chinese Classics:*
Vol. I, containing *The Confucian Analects, The Great Learning,* and *The Doctrine of the Mean.*
Vol. II, *The Works of Mencius.*
Vol. III (Part I and II), containing the *Shooking.*
Vol. IV (Part I and II), containing the *Sheking.*
Vol. V (Part I and II), containing Dukes Yin Hwan, Chwang, Min, He, Wan, Seuen and Ch'ing and the *Prolegomena,* Dukes Seang Ch'aou, Ting and Sae with Tso's *Appendix.* Oxford, 1893.

BIBLIOGRAPHY

Legge, James, *The Sacred Books of China. The Texts of Confucianism.* Oxford, 1879.

—— *Confucianism in Relation to Christianity.* A Paper read before the Missionary Conference in Shanghai, 1877. Shanghai and London, 1877.

Müller, F. Max, *The Religions of China. I. Confucianism. Nineteenth Century,* Vol. XLVIII, September, 1900.

Strauss, V. v., *Schi-king.* Heidelberg, 1880.

Tschepe, P. A., *Heiligtümer des Konfuzianismus in K'ü-fu and Tschou-Hien mit 63 Illustr. und 3 Karten.* Yentschoufu, Kath. Mission, 1906.

—— *Konfuzius (1. Sein Leben; 2. Seine Schüler).* Yentschoufu, 1910-1915.

Uno, Tetsuto, *Die Ethik des Konfuzianismus.* Berlin, Japaninstitut, 1927.

Wang Ching-dao, *Confucius and New China. Confucius' Idea of the State and its relation to the constitutional government.* Shanghai, Commercial Press, 1912.

Wilhelm, Richard, *K'ung-Tse. Leben und Werk.* Stuttgart, Frommann, 1925.

—— *K'ungfutse Gespräche (Lun Yü).* Jena, 1921.

—— *I Ging. Das Buch der Wandlungen.* Jena, 1924.

—— *Mong Dsï.* Jena, 1921.

—— *Chinesische Lebensweisheit.* Darmstadt, 1922.

Williams, E. T., *The State Religion of China during the Manchu dynasty. Journ. N.C.B.R. As. Soc.,* Vol. XLIV. 1913.

Zenker, E. V., *Geschichte der chinesischen Philosophie.* I. Reichenberg, 1926.

Supplementary Bibliography Added
by the Translators

Chavannes, Edouard, *Les Mémoires historiques de Se-Ma Ts'ien traduits et annotés*. Paris, 1905.

Franke, O., *Geschichte des chinesischen Reiches, Eine Darstellung seiner Entstehung, seines Wesens und seiner Entwicklung bis zur neuesten Zeit. 1. Band, Das Altertum und das Werden des konfuzianischen Staates*. Berlin, Leipzig, 1930.

Granet, Marcel, *Danses et légendes de la Chine ancienne. Tome première*. Paris, 1926.

Henke, F. G., *The Philosophy of Wang Yang-ming*. Chicago, 1917.

Hu Shih, *The Development of the Logical Method in China*. Shanghai, 1928.

Liang Chi-chao, *History of Chinese Political Thought During the Early Tsin Period*. London, 1930.

Maspero, H., *La Chine ancienne*. Paris, 1925.

Müller, F. Max, *Sacred Books of the East*. Vols. III, IV, XVI, XXII. London, 1885.

Schindler, Bruno, *Das Priestertum im alten China*. Leipzig, 1919.

Steele, J., *The I Li*. Oxford, 1917.

Thomas, Elbert Duncan, *Chinese Political Thought: A study Based upon the Theories of the Principal Thinkers of the Chou Period*. New York, 1927.

SUPPLEMENTARY BIBLIOGRAPHY

Wilhelm, Richard, *Chinese Civilization* (translation). New York and London, 1929.

—— *Die Chinesische Philosophie.* Breslau, 1929.

—— *Dschuang Dsi.* Jena, 1920.

—— *Die Seele Chinas.* Berlin, 1926. (Transl. as *The Soul of China.* New York, 1928.)

Printed in the United States ·
136874LV00010B/30/A

9 781432 572211